To John with all
my best wishes

INNERFITNESS

Five Steps to Overcoming Fear and Anxiety While Building Your Self-Worth

NORDINE ZOUAREG
FORMER MR. UNIVERSE

Foreword by Dr. Richard Carmona

Skyhorse Publishing

Skyhorse Publishing books may be purchased in bulk at special discounts for sales promotion, corporate gifts, fund-raising, or educational purposes. Special editions can also be created to specifications. For details, contact the Special Sales Department, Skyhorse Publishing, 307 West 36th Street, 11th Floor, New York, NY 10018 or info@skyhorsepublishing.com.

Skyhorse® and Skyhorse Publishing® are registered trademarks of Skyhorse Publishing, Inc.®, a Delaware corporation.

Visit our website at www.skyhorsepublishing.com.

10 9 8 7 6 5 4 3 2 1

Library of Congress Cataloging-in-Publication Data is available on file.

Cover design by Brian Peterson

InnerFitness is a registered trademark.
All clients who are referenced in this book have had their names changed to protect their identity.

Print ISBN: 978-1-5107-5741-7
Ebook ISBN: 978-1-5107-5742-4

Printed in the United States of America

I dedicate this book to those who will take the journey to health and wellness; those who found inner peace in the mist of chaos and challenging times. And to those who have the courage to rise above.

To my mother, Yamina, and to my loving children, Samir, Samira, Tarek, Walid, Armand, and Isabella.

CONTENTS

Foreword by Dr. Richard Carmona   *v*

Introduction: Regaining Inner Peace   *vii*

PART I: RECLAIMING YOUR SELF-WORTH

Chapter One: Self-Esteem: Society's Addiction   1

Chapter Two: Just Take the Leap   11

Chapter Three: The Five Issues   19

Chapter Four: Self-Worth   23

Chapter Five: Trust   45

Chapter Six: Tranquility   55

PART II: SYNERGY: YOUR MIND, BODY, AND SPIRIT CONNECTION

Chapter Seven: Body   75

Chapter Eight: The Four Pillars of Mindful Fitness   89

Chapter Nine: Golden Rule #1: Sleep   105

Chapter Ten: Golden Rule #2: Breathe   121

Chapter Eleven: Golden Rule #3: Eat   133

Chapter Twelve: Golden Rule #4: Move   159

Chapter Thirteen: Golden Rule #5: Yoga   177

Epilogue: Don't Give Up: "Desire to Fight"   *183*

Author's Note Pertaining to COVID-19   *193*

Acknowledgments   *198*

FOREWORD

InnerFitness is a timely and much-needed addition to a nation struggling with mounting preventable physical and mental challenges that require new and innovative approaches.

As we put 2020 behind us, we approach 2021 as an unwell world. An infectious disease pandemic potentiating a mental health pandemic in a nation plagued by hyper partisan politics being viewed by a world witnessing democracy being challenged. All of the aforementioned being superimposed on an unwell nation already saddled with an increasing preventable disease and economic burden.

A tsunami of self-help books, podcasts, and apps have emerged to address whatever your self-diagnosed chief complaint may be. However, addressing your chief complaint without understanding the holistic underlying relationship to your self-identified problem is like trying to extinguish a fire while fire accelerants are being added.

Fortunately, Nordine Zouareg, author and international fitness and wellness expert, realized that a broader health philosophy was needed. He has now built on his previously successful 2007 publication *Mind Over Body*, and has provided us with his renewed guidance in *InnerFitness*.

Nordine has not only written about the essential mind-body connection for optimizing health and wellness, as well as including weight loss, but he actually embodies these concepts in his daily life activities. He has been recognized as Mr. France, Mr. Europe, and Mr. Universe in global body building competitions.

In *InnerFitness*, he defines how we are inextricably tied to our mental health status and mindset and that finding our inner peace is essential for fitness and health.

In six opening chapters, Nordine outlines an approach to reclaiming your self-worth, followed by seven more chapters explaining the importance of connecting mind, body, and spirit.

InnerFitness is essentially the proven life plan and experiences of a very successful fitness entrepreneur. Unlike many books and testimonials, Nordine "walks the talk" and speaks from personally applying evolving science to his life to achieve a desired outcome which, in his case, was being recognized as the best in the world.

Although Nordine personally took this information to the maximal limit, he has written this book in a very practical and easy to read manner so the average person can greatly benefit as well. Achieving optimal inner fitness is dependent on aligning mind, body, and spirit.

Nordine has provided us the needed path forward.

Richard H. Carmona, M.D., M.P.H., FACS
17th Surgeon General of the United States

INTRODUCTION

REGAINING INNER PEACE

Don't let failure or success affect your inner peace.

FOR ALL OF us in our lives, there are times when we experience deep levels of fear, anxiety, doubt, or even depression. Things fall apart, and we seem to have no way of bringing ourselves back to peace. Such challenges as unmanaged stress at work, overwhelming life changes, or unfortunate losses emerge out of nowhere. We feel the incredible pressure of those difficult situations and it throws us off balance as we're not prepared, not strong enough, or simply don't know how to deal with them. Inner peace becomes then an ever-elusive fantasy—it has lost its true meaning.

We have a mental health crisis. Passionless, unworthy, unlovable, and insufficient is how we mostly feel—and we don't want to talk about it mainly because of the stigma attached to our predicament. We'd rather be safe and keep on faking it by wearing our mask of deception—to some of us, this delusion can last a lifetime. I call this living at a low and dangerous level of existence, where reality is no longer available to us.

Like most people, and for a long time, I thought to reach inner peace I had to have peace of mind first—by thinking about, doing, achieving, and gaining the things that would lead me there. Success, achievement, fame, and money weren't bringing me peace, they pushed me away from it, and the more I got the more I wanted—I was only feeding my self-esteem. My ego.

Luckily, they also helped me realize that I was forgetting about the part of me that would make the difference: my inner being, which is the very foundation for the creation of everything, including inner peace. Imagine being engaged in creating your deepest desires without being attached to the outcome—you are creating while being in the here and now, with no fear of failure or success. This approach helped me tremendously; it allowed me to find the strength to stop looking for peace in my head. It is there that I graciously stumbled upon the awareness of my delusion. I immediately understood that staying at the level of the mind would further create difficulties for others and myself. I knew that no matter what was happening to me, there was more than the physical body, the fame, or the thoughts that were going through my head. To diffuse any tension that would arise from any situation, I would have to go beyond the fallacious belief that peace was of the mind—a concept held by many from the beginning of time. Although God placed love in the human heart, it's the last place he'd search for it.

Peace Is Not of the Mind

Peace is not of the mind. It's beyond its confine, and you won't find it if you keep looking in all the wrong places—in your job, your relationships, your dreams, your physical appearance, or everywhere else. Peace is within you! It's a comfortable space surrounded by an uncomfortable world—like a lotus that has its roots in the mud but remains beautiful and strong. When you connect with your inner peace, you step through a door in time and into a new reality where you conceive without the fear of losing it all—you're not attached to the outcome. You have ultimate freedom from ego; you cease to be in a state of constant lack and are in control of your life.

To illustrate this concept, I request you do a simple exercise: sit comfortably on a chair (or whatever you are sitting on), close your eyes, and take a few slow and deep breaths. Now project your mind back in time. Reflect on a situation that recently caused you to be negative, perhaps even angry.

How do you feel now? Probably as negative and as angry as when it first happened, right? Even though the event has already taken place, you're still experiencing the same emotions. That's what the mind does!

Now pay attention to your breathing, allow it to bring you back to the present moment. Use this exercise as a portal to mindfulness—remember that every time you pay attention to your breathing, you are connecting to the present moment. How do you feel now? Peaceful, I bet! That's presence! That's peace! And that is *not* in your mind! It's in the deepest part of you; it's in your being. Let's bring this into further focus. Let's take your body, for instance; it has always existed in the present moment, not in the "yesterday" or in the "tomorrow." To my knowledge, no one has ever physically touched their body in the past or the future. Your body is always here, in the now.

To quote the British philosopher Alan W. Watts:

We seem to be driven along by our past. We believe that life is moving under the power of the past but that's another fallacy, the past is the present. We don't realize that the true reality in which we live is the present moment, the now. We spend most of our time and a great deal of our emotional energy living in time which is not here, living in an "elsewhere" which appears to be illusory.

It's in your mind's nature to keep taking you into the past or the future. It runs wild, like an untamed stallion. It generates turmoil and unnecessary suffering, and is excellent at making you believe that you are not enough, that you need more, or are constantly under threat. That's inner conflict! Your state of mind battles with your state of being; your thoughts are clashing with the way you want to feel. You want peace but feel anxious, angry, or frustrated because of obsessive and toxic negative thinking. Your mind is taking you on a merry-go-round. Why does it do that? Well, it's a primal human instinct—we all have it, and it's not going anywhere. It wants to protect itself from danger. Except, in this case, the imaginary tiger is not chasing you—it's *you* that's chasing you! Your body is here, but your mind is elsewhere. Even when you succeed in "getting there"—you get the job or the promotion—you want to be elsewhere. *You are never here! You are not at peace!*

We have always been here in this moment. And so have you!

Take the family that waits years before they go on their dream vacation—Paris has been on their minds since dad brought up the idea. They finally can afford to make that dream a reality. The trip is amazing; mostly captured on camera and shared on social media. Ten days later, they're back home and while watching videos and viewing photos of their journey, they realize that most of what they've captured on film they haven't truly enjoyed or even seen other than from behind the camera—they were too busy capturing, editing, posting, etc. They weren't fully present—they weren't there—and that, my friends, is a tragedy!

Unfortunately, this is how most human beings live their lives—they hide behind the lenses of fear, doubt, and anxiety. They are afraid to enjoy their lives fully engaged, fully present, with no attachment to the outcome. This is not the same as to say that one shouldn't practice visualization to manifest one's heart's desires, but an attempt to debunk the belief that one needs to cling to something or someone to attain happiness. I love to achieve things, but I never cling to them as I've learned the hard way—as you may have read or will discover later in this book.

To regain inner peace, we must eliminate inner conflicts. We must learn how to stop spending so much energy living a low level of existence by desperately trying to seek validation from others—our bosses, our friends, our partners, or even total strangers.

Peace Is *Not* on Social Media

It's not surprising that almost *half* of the planet's population is addicted to technology, social media, fake news, and a fake sense of self. Even big companies and political campaigns spend millions of dollars on social media ads targeting their prospects through well-crafted and extremely captivating slogans using self-esteem as bait . . . and it works! Facebook earned $16.6 billion in advertising revenue for the second quarter of 2019. Mind-boggling numbers! And with social media marketing, no matter what the message is—ill or well intended—it influences people's convictions or beliefs so they can *do* or *want* more of something.

A recent report published by the Royal Society for Public Health in the UK examined the effects of social media on young people's mental health. Their findings show a clear picture of how different social media platforms impacted mental health issues, including depression, anxiety, sleep deprivation, and body image. According to the report, Instagram appeared to have the most negative effect on that population's mental health and well-being.

The photo-sharing app negatively impacted body image and sleep quality, increased bullying and "FOMO" (fear of missing out), and led to greater feelings of anxiety, depression, and loneliness. The positive effects included self-expression, self-identity, community building, and emotional support via positive feedback.

Undoubtedly, social media has its place in this fast-paced society—it's a force to reckon with—but only if it inspires, educates, and elevates the masses. We must, however, not ignore the undeniable fact that social media platforms can be also used—as we've seen—to destabilize entire countries, influence the outcome of an election, intimidate, and spread fake news.

Furthermore, mental health issues are on the rise. In fact, according to the World Health Organization (WHO), the United States is now the world's most affected country. These days, there is an enormous pressure to impress, and it's easy to get caught up comparing yourself to other people's highlight reel. It's gotten so bad that young people are committing self-harm and staging their own suicide on social media platforms. The CDC estimates that 50 percent of Americans will be diagnosed with a mental illness or disease in their lifetime, and mental illnesses are now the third most common cause of hospitalization in the US for people aged eighteen to forty-four. As you'll learn later in this book, the doctor's office or the emergency room were often the only place where I'd find reassurance.

The numbers of people that like or dislike you don't really matter—it is the amount of love you have for yourself that does. We are like magnets—we attract what we project.

There's no doubt that this is a crisis, and we need to stop stigmatizing mental illness and have a more open discussion around mental health. In this book, I offer powerful tools for eliminating inner conflicts and regaining inner peace. Trust me, I have been there, and I am sure that most of you who are reading this book have been, too. You know it's a very lonely place.

Back in the Day

Growing up, we didn't have all this craziness. Based on status, whether economic or even racial background, different circumstances troubled us. Those circumstances often made me feel compelled to throw in the towel and give up on my goals and dreams. But I realized that to overcome the physical and emotional pain inflicted by the beatings, the bullies at school, the humiliating defeats in competitions, and the racists who terrorized my family, I had to go inward, climb the pole, and rise above; learn to stay focused on my objectives. I knew I'd stay at the bottom of the pole if I kept blaming myself and seeking answers elsewhere, other than within me. Believing in myself and staying true to my dreams kept my faith strong and my will indestructible. I remember that sometimes life hit me so hard I felt I'd never get back up, so I'd just curl up in my bed and hide from the outside world. But there was something greater than my fear that always pulled me up: self-worth.

Self-worth, not self-esteem, became my gateway with the divine; it helped me find inner peace. It transcended my self-esteem, which was often the trigger to my challenges. It is the spark that brought the light back to my life. Fueled by the desire to fight and win, I'd learned to take hard punches from life and throw some back. When I reminisce on my past, I'm often reminded of an excellent part in the movie *Rocky Balboa*—the last installment in the *Rocky* series. In it, Rocky is attempting to inspire his son Robert, who seems to hide behind his father's boxing accomplishments and fame. Rocky is attempting to get his son out of that "Don't you care what people think?" mindset—a low-esteem issue brought up by the fear of not being enough. He explains that life is hard, and it takes courage and extraordinary strength to take responsibility for your mistakes and stop blaming others—stop dancing to the tune of others' drumbeats and go after your own dreams. My best quote of that part of the movie is when Rocky spills his guts and screams:

> It ain't about how hard you can hit, it's about how hard you can get hit and keep moving forward. How much you can take and keep moving forward. That's how winning is done. Now if you know what you're

worth, go out and get what you're worth. But you gotta be willing to take the hits and stop pointing fingers.

I want you to pay close attention to the last part of the quote: *"Now if you know what you're worth, go out and get what you're worth."* Notice the emphasize on self-worth—Rocky is talking about worth as accomplishments, God-given abilities, dreams, goals, all the things that one truly desires despite what others think and without their approval. That's self-worth! There's only one thing I would change in this spirited discussion, however, instead of saying: *"Go get what you're worth!"*—I'd say: *"Reclaim what's truly yours!"* Since you don't get self-worth, it's innate; you're born with it—it's your birthright! So, if we keep thinking self-worth is *out there*, it becomes deceptive and much harder to connect to, therefore often confusing it with self-esteem, which is wordily rather than soul filling.

I know now that every hit I took was a lesson to learn, and every lesson learned a step toward success. When things went bad, I would just let it pass like a bad storm. Eventually, the rain would stop. Rising up, reevaluating my purpose, readjusting my goals, and keeping my eyes on the prize have empowered me to move on. It kept me moving forward! Challenge is part of success. Without it, there would be no desire to fight for what you believe. It's by experiencing inner conflict that I came to discover inner peace and create my state of InnerFitness. One after the other, I jumped the hurdles and got to the victory lane. Like I said, the path might be long and arduous, but the harder it gets the sweeter the victory.

This Book

This isn't your usual self-help book. For starters, it doesn't tell you what to do. It doesn't force you to take three steps every day so you can feel refreshed. It doesn't yell at you to become a badass and conquer the world. It asks, instead, that you reclaim an important power you have as a human being—choice. It asks you to listen, dig deep, and find the courage to empower yourself. If you want to steer your own destiny, the key is choice. All of us want to outlive our past, live in the present, and take control of the future. The only way we can do that is by being intentional about the decisions we make. Choices are the building blocks and foundation of a successful and contented lifestyle. My clients, when they are standing on a pole 40 feet high, are simulating how difficult it can be to make decisions. The slow, excruciating climb up is all of us dealing with the emotional turmoil a particular fork in the road can cause. It can be emotionally and physically exhausting to try and overcome all the noise clouding your head. But if you want to step up and capture your potential and live life to the fullest, you need to have the strength to face and make the smallest and biggest choices. You need to take the leap and create an optimum state of InnerFitness.

The Field of Possibilities

I didn't have a heart attack. I should have been relieved, but I wasn't. The doctor was explaining to me that I had just suffered a panic attack. Me, a healthy forty-year-old, husband, father of two, and a fitness director at one of the top spas in the world, was suffering from crippling anxiety. At first, doctors and nurses thought I was faking it. It didn't help that this was my third trip to the emergency room in the past couple of months. It was hard for me to explain to them how real my attacks felt. My heart beating a mile a minute, gasping for air, feeling like my soul was being sucked out of me, and the emptiness after the attack passed. To be honest, I didn't understand what I was going through. How could my body act like I was dying when nothing was physically wrong with me? The doctor recommended I go see a psychiatrist, and I eagerly complied. I hated how I felt and wanted to be well again. After a very short meeting with the psychiatrist—who wasn't particularly interested in my story or my concerns—he prescribed Xanax. Maybe medication does help people, but my experience was different. On Xanax, the world slowed down around me. I felt like I was walking through water. Nothing felt vibrant anymore. Life was dull and boring. My world got small and narrow and was shrinking in front of my eyes.

Later I understood that my anxiety was clearly just a symptom. I was going through a life-changing shift, which I didn't realize at the time. Everything had ground to a halt for me. I had a prestigious job, I was a good father and hus-band, but I had given in to all of my fears. They were crowding out my joy, productivity, and putting a stop to achieving my goals and dreams. It was clear I was holding onto emotional baggage that was dragging me down. I couldn't break out of negative thinking patterns and habits. All the advice and tools I had learned before weren't helping. I had gotten through life by faking it until I made it. Now it became clear faking it just meant *faking it* and nothing more. There also was no way to release my anger, fears, and sadness. They were stored in my body and making me physically ill. So not only was I emotionally drained, but also physically. There was no will left in me to change the situation.

This is when I came across this Deepak Chopra quote: "You and I are essen-tially infinite choice makers. In every moment of our existence, we are in that field of possibilities where we have access to an infinity of choices."

There is so much truth in his words. As human beings, the universe has offered us the gift of choice. With just one decision, we can change the course of our life. But, often, there's something stopping us. It could be doubt, fear, intense worry, and desire to delay and self-sabotage. For me, personally, there was always an excuse handy. I used my anxiety as an excuse to stop living. I was willingly giving up my power of choice and placing my destiny in the hands of fate, the whims of other people, and my negative mindset. Even when I was ready to express my power of choice and take back control of my destiny, I still had to unearth the emotions and thinking patterns that were holding me back. As I dug into my psyche, I realized it wasn't just my anxiety.

For the past decade, I have been helping my clients harness their power of choice. It's something we don't think very much about, but if you want to have a contented and happy life, you need to embrace your existence in the field of possibilities. If you don't, all the infinite choices offered by the universe will be wasted. And, from personal experience, I can tell you, you will live an unin-spired life. In this book—and despite the conventional belief that they're the same—I begin with exposing the myth of self-esteem and highlighting the importance of the most fundamental core belief: that self-worth is the foundation of every action and decision in life. Without curating and cultivating self-worth, I will show you, dear reader, how you will feel empty and lack the necessary drive and fuel to take advantage of infinite choices. With self-worth as your solid foundation, you will know how to build trust, maintain calm, protect your body, and create a "desire to fight." By using stories from my own life and client success stories, I will offer the blueprint so you never cower from making decisions or choices that will change your life for the better.

Part I

Reclaiming Your Self-Worth

CHAPTER ONE

SELF-ESTEEM:
SOCIETY'S ADDICTION

There's always something or someone you'll compare yourself to—it will either make you feel good or bad—such is the law of self-esteem. The problem for many people then is that they've become so used to looking outward for validation and satisfaction that they've lost touch with their ability to look inward.

MOST OF US ARE being bombarded by society's requirements to fit a certain image, a certain mold, and adapt to a certain way of life. We are being dictated the way we should be and how we should behave based on "self-*esteem*"—which comes from the Latin word *aestimare* ("to estimate"). At any time, someone can make us feel so small or hugely important by making an estimation of who we appear to be based on *their* perception of us. Perceptions are mere subjective observations and are largely influenced by one's subconscious programming—and often hidden agenda. Essentially, they are unable to truly identify or capture another person's thoughts or feelings. Emotional inferiority or superiority are at the core of self-esteem—and therefore are very deceptive. When you are comparing yourself with someone else, you are making a deceitful estimation of who they should be because you don't know the half of it; you only see the façade others like to show you. Low or high, self-esteem is just that—an estimation based on the external aspects of one's life. It is always short-lived and ego-based—someone or something can make you feel either *bad* or *good*—by telling you what you want to hear or what they want you to hear. Trust me, growing up I had my share of school bullies—classmates and teachers alike—beating and making me feel so worthless that I didn't want to live anymore. I had low self-esteem. It was like walking around with a board that had "Beat me up, I'm worthless!" written on it. Be careful what you wish for!

But I also had many admiring fans. The many victories, the autograph sessions, the book signings, working with celebrities, all that felt amazing. It felt so exhilarating that I got addicted. Just like in a roller-coaster ride, my confidence would go up and down, depending on the praise, victory, or critic. It's so strange that self-esteem drives most human beings. I see it every day and pretty much everywhere I go, but the gym seems to be the place with lots of pumped-up self-esteems; most people there seem to emphasize the physical aspect rather than health itself.

The obsession with buns of steel and six packs is what I'm referring to. They have taken front row in this new and short-lived superficial happiness fueled by social media and backed by the ego-based self-esteem. As I reference multiple times in this book, to create harmony in everything we do one must align body, mind, and spirit. It is when we are off balance or out of alignment that we fail to create long-lasting peace and well-being. I, too, was obsessed with my body image, and for a long time I was living and breathing bodybuilding. But I became aware of the emotional pain it was causing me and the people I loved. I realized, after many years of hard work, that I wasn't only building a strong body but also creating an invisible armor that would shield me from an unresolved issue with my low self-esteem. Eventually, I had to face my issue and relinquish my ego-driven obsession—I surrendered to the idea that my body is a strong and beautiful external expression of who I am and cannot exist without the union of the other two—mind and spirit. When one lives and thrives on others' admiration, one becomes addicted to external stimuli. Therefore, one ceases to experience true inspiration, and inner peace is jeopardized.

To further solidify my point, I want you to recall the feeling you have when someone praises, accepts, or applauds you—which comes from external stimuli and can be very motivating. And compare that with the feeling that arises within you when you look into the eyes of a child, or look up at the sunset, climb a mountain, or even when you read an inspiring book or watch a movie you enjoy. How do you feel? Inspired? That's right, it's soul-driven . . . which comes from within.

Want vs. Need: A Difference You Must Grasp

I thought I'd start this section with the definitions of the words *want* and *need* respectively:

Want: To have a desire to possess or do (something); wish for.

Need: Require (something) because it is essential or very important.

We live in a culture where almost the entire economy depends on targeting people's self-esteem—by making them feel a fake sense of happiness, thus craving more productivity, thrill, pleasure, and excitement. These feelings don't produce the sustenance and happiness that's felt when one walks in nature or enjoys the company of one's friends or family members. Those who are controlled by these emotions spend every minute of their waking lives seeking them. This is a dangerous phenomenon and the leading contributor to unhappiness, discontent, inner conflict, and the delivery system for such controlling force is self-esteem; a misleading concept that society has harnessed and used against billions to influence or challenge their beliefs, perceptions, emotions, and feelings since its discovery in 1619.

Research has shown that people buy or do things they want; things that make them feel happy or feel better about themselves—not necessarily because they need them. Our society has created the superficiality of wanting things we don't need. We feel that we have to measure up to those around us, to keep up with the Joneses, have the biggest and nicest house, fanciest car, trendiest clothes, or the most expansive wedding. Although there is nothing wrong with indulging in the things we want as our finances allow—and as long as we don't get attached or link our happiness to them—it's always a good idea to identify the cause that's triggering the impulsive behavior; wanting to do or buy things just to fit in.

A very good example of this phenomenon is the iPhone. Apple has created a genius trend around its product that, as soon as they launch the device, people will show up at the Apple stores in droves—sometimes even sleeping at storefronts the night before. People have to have the new model no matter what, even if the old one works. It makes them feel better and boosts their self-esteem— they have their toy before anyone else has. Trust me, I know. I have teenagers, and I must confess that I've done it, too—maybe not the sleeping part, but the waiting part. The thrill lasted about two hours. I often wondered about the rationality of such behavior. Why do we buy things we don't need? Could boredom and the lack of mindfulness have anything to do with this, and cause us to want things? We often find reasons to justify our actions by literally lying to ourselves for the sake of feeling better about something we knew, deep down, we shouldn't have done? Or could it be because of the immediate gratification or pleasure—the release of dopamine in the brain—our wanting always seems to outweigh the reckoning of suffering the consequences of resisting the urge? Researchers have long shown that the link between shopping and addiction is not a myth, but a reality.

One thing's for sure, most of us rationalize and come up with motives or excuses for why we do what we do—in this case, buying stuff. This perpetual inner conflict between our "selves"—the one that wants and the one that needs—will continue until we gain awareness of its existence. The question to ask then is: "Do I want it, or do I need it?" This is obviously easier said than done. Well, what if I told you that *wanting* always comes from the ego—it feeds off it! If you don't believe me, look in your wardrobe and you'll see what I'm referring to. Do you really need all those pairs of shoes or all those suits?

Again, there's nothing wrong with wanting to have stuff, provided that you are not clinging to them. Notice the key word here is *clinging*. One must learn not to confuse happiness with gratification, accomplishments, gain, or satisfaction. This is not only limited to the stuff we buy, but the same thing also applies to the superficial relationships we entertain, the jobs we choose, or the gossips we spread around . . . it makes us feel important. Being authentic and honest is paramount to finding your way to inner peace. Ultimately, you must look into your heart and do what you know is right.

Self-esteem motivates but doesn't inspire—it's mostly driven by external stimuli. Your stream of thoughts creates it. When you tell yourself you can't do this or that or that you're not enough, that's coming from your mind; your ego is talking to you.

Money Can't Buy Happiness . . . or Can It?

I both agree and disagree when it comes to the following statement: "Money can't buy happiness." In 1750, Rousseau wrote: "Money can buy material things, but real happiness must be truly earned."

It's true that money is one way—not the only way—to get you what you want; to live the life of your dreams. I will never dispute that. But what I will say is that happiness is not a state of mind, but rather a state of being. You can't get it from another, you can't give it to another, you can't buy it and can't find it other than within yourself. If money could buy happiness, no one on this planet would be happy (other than the 1 percent).

Superficial happiness is what I refer to when people seek it by doing or collecting things or even expecting it from others. When I describe superficial happiness, I like to compare love and fear and how to identify when ego poses as love. Ego is always wanting and is conditional—"I am happy only when I get this or that!" or "I can't live without you!" You usually catch it when an attachment or clinging arises. Love is unconditional and never rushes to someone or something to fill your emptiness—no attachment there. Mindfulness seems to be love's main attribute. Ego is always sponsored by fear.

My father was an illiterate, hard-working blue-collar man. He was broke most of the time, yes, but not poor. His holiness, the Dalai Lama, lives on ten dollars a day—by choice. He is not poor; he is happy . . . not superficially so, and for no particular reason. If you define happiness in terms of people, things, or accolades, you'll never truly experience it. Instead, you'll create unhappiness. What's the difference? Well happiness, as I said before, is a state of being you connect to. Unhappiness is a state of mind you automatically engage to when you think negative thoughts and manifest new problems for yourself. I agree that, yes, when you have lots of money, you can give some to the underprivileged—the homeless, or people in need—you're able to help, it satis-fies their hunger or needs but will not make them happy. And how do you even know if they're unhappy? Judging by their appearance would be a great mistake.

I've been volunteering at the H. S. Lopez Family Foundation Center of Opportunity, a homeless shelter and recovery service that was formerly a hotel and conference center in Tucson, Arizona. Every Sunday, when I'm in town, I help serve lunch to the underprivileged. I honestly can't tell you if one is happier than the other. What I can tell you however is that feeding and sheltering them is only one aspect of what could make them feel happy. We can contribute to someone's happiness by helping them in any way we can but, ultimately, it's up to the individual to find alignment in their lives. They can be happy one moment and unhappy the next. Just like life, happiness is a moment-to-moment equilibrium. Coming to grasp with this undeniable concept will save you from unnecessary pain and suffering. It will bring you one step closer to inner peace. And I, for one, always believed that happiness was something you get . . . boy, was I wrong.

You Are Your Own Worst Enemy

When I was first hired as a fitness and wellness director at the world-renowned resort spa Miraval in August 1999, I couldn't imagine the place was even in Tucson. The resort looked very much like a sanctuary; a paradise located right at the foot of the Santa Catalina Mountains filled with palm trees and all kinds of cactuses. The breathtaking landscape reminded me very much of Bou Saada, an oasis before entering the Sahara Desert in Algeria, about seven miles from where I was born.

As part of Miraval's efforts to compete with the industry's top resorts, I was asked to create a new and unique fitness department with programs and classes that emphasized mindfulness, which was (and still is) the resort's motto.

I have to be honest with you. In 1999, the fitness industry was anything but mindful; to describe it, only one word comes to mind, *obsession*. I believe if it weren't for a handful of my colleagues, specifically Joseph Denucci, a staunch ally and also the resort's CEO, who was convinced that I was the guy he needed to make it happen, I wouldn't have been able to achieve this monumental task. *Who's better than a former Mr. Universe who practices yoga and meditation to come up with the perfect program?* He one's uttered during a staff meeting. Those words boosted my confidence and self-esteem, I must confess, and they also fueled my obsession to get the job done; thus helping in creating an award-winning resort spa and wellness programs, thanks to all the staff then and now.

But for me, it all came at a heavy price.

I was relentless and steadfast in my resolve to succeed. But, deep down, I was terrified. I didn't think I had it in me; I was intimidated and afraid to deceive. Sadly, it was a recurring self-belief since childhood. So with my fear hidden by superficial enthusiasm and driven by Joseph's conviction—which boosted my self-esteem—I began my journey and embarked on a path to victory. I used the same discipline I'd use in high-level competition the previous years, except I wasn't only using passion as fuel this time. Fear became my daily companion and I buried myself in work. I was determined to win the respect of those who were questioning my competence and ability to get the job done while being driven by the trust of those who had faith in me. Attached to the wonderful accolades, however—as I experienced the phenomenon many times over by winning several world titles—came the stress and worry of living up to new fame.

Unfortunately, and as you will soon discover in this book, fear can drain your energy and kill your creativity if you let it. It did just that to me! At one point, and as a direct result of self-inflicted and unnecessary stress, I got so inefficient at managing my time and energy that I was literally forced by upper management to use my days off. In hindsight, I had relinquished control over my personal life and lived by someone else's perception of who I was. It didn't matter how bad or how good the perception was, it was just a perception; a false belief generated by another's own fear and hidden agenda.

Although I worked at a spa whose famous approach was *mindfulness*, and who's reputation for helping guests find inner peace was unmatched, I was out of sync with the message. The more I did—creating programs, teaching classes, speaking, conducting one-on-one consultations, managing, etc.—the more I had to worry about . . . I was losing control over something I built and came to love. I suffered from stress and anxiety and was feeling overwhelmed. I had difficulties identifying the source of my angst. I wasn't sure if the stress was causing my anxiety or if it was my fear of "not being good enough" that did. Although I was achieving a lot, I felt unhappy—I was like a mouse running in circles. Fortunately, the universe has a rather strange way to stop you in your track to self-destruction; it sends you little warnings in the form of messages and if you keep ignoring them, it'll send you a major reminder. I received mine one Christmas Eve in 2003.

Message Received

When the universe speaks you have to listen.

Maybe it's a recurring dream, a thought, a physical pain, or an injury—read the message and apply its content. I often neglected the messages the universe sent me and I often had to suffer the consequences of such doing.

It was cold and very muddy that day and, as usual, I was leaving the office late. In a hurry to get home to my wife, Keri, my one-month-old baby, Isabella, and my eighteen-month-old toddler, Armand, who were expecting me for dinner, I slipped and fell. *No, not me!* I thought to myself, laying there and unable to get up after a failed attempt that worsened the agony. It's both scary and fascinating how the brain can remember a traumatic event as if it happened five minutes ago. "It's a ruptured patella tendon, and it's a very serious injury, we need to operate!," Ty Endean, a prominent orthopedic surgeon who served on the medical staff for the Oakland Raiders, exclaimed. To confirm the diagnosis, I had an MRI done and had surgery three days later—it was a successful operation as expected. But that freak accident was also one of those defining moments.

Overwhelmed by the fear of losing everything—my job, our new house, our cars, and all that comes with a comfortable family life—coupled with the excruciating pain and confined to a couch with my leg elevated, I reflected upon my life situation. The universe had succeeded! It delivered its message, and I received it! But how was I going to translate this ever-enigmatic dilemma? As fear, doubt, and frustration were consuming my every thought, I wasn't able to make sense of my unfortunate situation. I was still in shock. How could this happen to me? I've competed at a highly competitive level and worked out all my life—lifted the equal of four thousand loaded semi-trucks and ran about twenty-six thousand miles—yet it took one fall to bring me down.

This protective shield I displayed for more than 20 years had collapsed, and I could no longer hide behind that strong and chiseled body. I felt vulnerable. My American dream had become a nightmare, bringing me to the lowest level of existence where I was mentally, emotionally, and physically stuck, as well as spiritually disconnected. Even the medication the surgeon prescribed for the pain couldn't help induce (as they often do) that powerful sense of euphoria and help calm the voices in my head. And as long as I allowed those voices to haunt me, I was hopeless. Mild depression, anxiety, fear, and doubt were my closest companions, and I was in danger of falling deeper into hopelessness. But, ironically, the immobilization that caused by the injury also allowed me the time to reflect upon my life.

It then dawned to me that perhaps I was faking it—how could I be a pretending to teach guests how to balance their own life, when mine was anything but? I was faced with a conundrum; I realized that I wasn't walking the talk. I sacrificed too much, missed my kids' school plays, sports practices, birthdays, visits to family abroad, and important family dinners to name just a few. I had no time for friends and no social life. Ironically, I wasn't living a *life in balance*. It's at that moment that it hit me—I had reached a state of inner conflicts. Afraid of disappointing, I wanted to do *more*, but my obsession with work brought me even *less*, less happiness, less passion, and less life. I didn't feel at peace; I was off balance. Despite my athletic ability and physical appearance, I was spiritually unfit; I didn't have InnerFitness. Between yoga, meditation, equine activities, mindful eating and more, I had all the tools, all the experts I needed to regain calm and serenity right there in front of me, but I wasn't using them. *I let the fear of failure disrupt my inner peace.*

Upon reflecting on my self-inflicted and self-destructive thinking pattern, I *chose* to deal with my inner crisis and regain inner peace. I was ready to fight, take control, and reclaim my sanity—hence creating harmony between my mind and my body. It is then that I have begun my journey to climbing the pole towards a higher level of existence.

"When you stop confusing your job with who you are, you'll cease to be controlled by it and you'll discover freedom.

CHAPTER TWO

JUST TAKE THE LEAP

I take flight trusting that one day I will find peace within the chaos of my mind.

"**DO YOU ALL** feel calm? Do you all feel connected?"

A couple of people mutter, "Yes."

Standing in the center of a circle, I instruct everyone to take a deep breath.

"Good, look around and take it all in. The vastness around you is going to scare you."

There's nervous laughter.

A group of men and women have gathered around me in the deserts of Arizona. It's early morning, and everyone is enjoying the cool breeze before it starts to get hot. I motion them to follow me and take them on a short hike. It's the second day of the Create Your Optimum State of InnerFitness® workshop. Everyone has gotten to know each other and there is a lot of pleasant small talk. The group consists of executives, salespeople, and career high achievers who want to learn how to let go, surrender to their present, and experience mindfulness. I don't need to tell them what tension and anxiety feels like, they experience it every day. They are here because they don't want to feel these emotions day in and day out. After all, who could blame them? Up to this point, we've had a successful retreat. We had great group sessions, where we shared a lot of our fears and worries. A number of the participants told me they had breakthroughs and were able to realize what was motivating them to dwell in anxiety and tension. But on the second day, I could sense everyone was ready to go back. I could hear them saying, *I get it. I get it. Be present. Be mindful. Okay, I have things to do and places to be.* For most of them, this retreat was just another schedule on their calendar. It was something they could tick off on their to-do list and keep going.

We are at our destination. There are audible gasps.

"I don't know about this."

"Are you serious?"

I have to admit this is my favorite part of the retreat; I love seeing their shocked faces.

Surrounded by mountains, sparse greenery, and no trees, everyone can see the 40-foot-high telephone pole. Looking up at it, it seems to be slowly swaying in the wind.

"Okay, who wants to go first?"

A couple of hands go up. I invite them forward and get them all harnessed up. My instructions are very simple: "Listen to the voices in your head as you climb up and stand on the top. What are they saying to you?" The first person is Michael, a 250-pound, 6-foot-tall executive. He takes a deep breath and starts climbing up. About a third of the way up, he wavers and freezes for a bit. I can see his calf muscles tighten. But he composes himself and keeps climbing. It happens again as he gets closer to the top. This time, he takes a good three minutes before he resumes climbing. His final task is to stand on top of the pole. It takes him another five minutes or so to get his legs on the platform, then another two before he is able to stand up tall. I can see his legs shaking and a smile emerge on his face. We all give him a round of applause as he takes in the scenery.

"What do you want to do?" My voice echoes across the valley.

"Ahmm . . . I don't know. I don't know" he said, sounding slightly annoyed

"Okay, take your time. Listen to your voices."

"Are the ropes ready if I jump?"

"Yes, we are here for you. Whenever you are ready."

I can see him inch his way to the edge. He looks down and quickly looks away. He asks us again if we were ready. "Yes, of course," I reply. He jumps, while screaming, "I feel alive." His arms flailing, with his legs bicycling the air. But we catch him. As he comes down, I couldn't be prouder.

As a high performance and wellness coach, I have helped many people conquer the Quantum Leap Pole—an important icebreaker exercise in the retreat's program. I have seen and sensed the palpable fear of my clients as they stand at the bottom, looking up at the 40-foot-high telephone pole and at the top, when they are looking out into the vastness of the empty desert landscape, which can make them feel incredibly small and insignificant.

I can see on their faces all the emotions they are processing: fear, anxiety, anger, complete loss of control. The threat feels real. The wind can blow them off, and even though they have a harness, they still have a long drop to the bottom. But there's also elation. After making the decision to jump, the craziest things are yelled out: "I'm alive," "I'm not scared," "Free," "Happy." My favorites are the one-word screams. What I love about this exercise is that even though I have coached the workshop attendants through their emotions and fears beforehand, they are essentially on their own. They are the captain of their ship and can steer themselves however they want. Are they going to succumb to fear, the voices in their head, and anxiety? Are they going to decide it's too scary to jump?

Over the years, I have become fascinated by what the thought processes are at every stage of the jump. When I wait for them at the bottom, I take notice of their reactions. A lot of them can't make eye contact with me, which makes sense; it's a vulnerable and intimate experience they have just had. Others are elated and want to give me and everyone a hug and continue talking. The questions still linger, though: Where do they draw their strength from to take the leap? Why is it scary for some and invigorating for others? What kind of noise fills their head? Does it trigger past experiences?

All of us, at one point in our life, have stood on top of the pole wondering if we can make the decisions or choices that might turn our life around. *Can I start on the work project I have been putting off? What about the diet that will help me lose weight and get healthy? Can I save my marriage? What do I do after losing my job?*

My clients tell me that the hardest part is jumping. The fear can be overpowering. Sometimes I can see their entire body buckling under the pressure. What helps is that I can totally empathize.

Growing up, I lived in fear of my father, as well as teachers and bullies. For years, fear controlled my life.

The moment we are faced with a tough decision, we become aware of all the baggage we are constantly carrying around. I have seen how difficult and frightening it can be to make a choice; it stirs old emotions up. The angry father telling you to stop trying or the humiliation experienced at work or the utter loneliness of being far away from home. The noises come back to haunt you. With those in your head, you end up making one bad choice after another.

The Field of Definite Impossibilities

My own life is an example. By the age of twenty-four, I was a world champion bodybuilder, earning the titles of Mr. France, Mr. Europe, Mr. World, and Mr. Universe. I knew how to work my body to the limit and fight for my dreams.

However, my joy was momentary and my mind went to the next challenge or worry or fear, preparing for the next big fight. My body, mind, and soul were drained. I was a walking, talking, and functioning zombie.

It would make sense for me to give up, right? But this is when my animal instincts kicked in and my body, mind, and soul were ready for another fight. I was prepared to destroy everything around me by making reactive and impulsive decisions. And so, I ran away and moved to America, giving up my celebrity life. Only after the unexpected death of my father did I take a long, hard look at my own life and actively reflect on the emotions that affected my decisions.

As I mentioned earlier, a Deepak Chopra quote came to my rescue: "In every moment of our existence, we are in that field of possibilities where we have access to an infinity of choices."

In my life, I was taking myself out of the field of possibilities and entering what I call "the field of definite impossibilities," creating a prison where I was limiting my growth. A prison I built out of fear, anxiety, and a total lack of trust and self-worth. The failed businesses, romantic relationships, and other misfortunes all led me to my self-inflicted captivity. It's why I came up with my workshops and still continue to show my clients when they create their optimum state of InnerFitness, they are allowing themselves access to an infinite number of choices. When we stand frozen at the top, we are limiting our growth and our existence. To continue to be in the field of possibilities, we need to manage the voices and emotions that paralyze us.

When we let fear cloud our judgment, we relinquish happiness.

———

Time's up! It's 9:45 a.m. and we're about to start the Quantum Leap II. We've already allowed 15 minutes to gather everyone but there's still one missing person.

"I think we can start. Please don't wait for my husband, he's always late! Besides, I'm not sure he'll show up!" says Angela, a participant in one of my Create Your Optimum State of InnerFitness workshops taking place at Miraval Resort in Tucson, Arizona.

As we get ready to fit everyone with the proper safety gear, we hear someone screaming from a distance, "Wait, wait, I'm coming!" Somebody is running toward us, but we barely see the silhouette that's hidden within the beautiful and abundant landscape.

"I think that's him, that's Peter, my husband! I told you he's always late! It's embarrassing, I'm sorry!" Angela exclaims. "I didn't think he'd show up, he's afraid of everything."

It's not unusual to see late arrivals during events such as the Quantum Leap, as people often dread this challenging event.

"I'm so sorry, Nordine. I was on the phone with a client!" Peter utters as he arrives.

"OK, Peter, take a few deep breaths and relax."

I then hand him a small piece of paper and a pen—as I do for every participant—and instruct him to write the three fears that had hindered him from living his best life. I can't help but think these two will be a fun pair.

"Why are you late? I told you to shut the damn phone off! Hurry you're embarrassing me," Angela shouts with a reprimanding tone.

"I'm sorry! I had to take care of this client," Peter explains.

"OK, guys, we need to start so let's get fitted." I instruct everyone.

It took another 15 minutes to get all six participants geared up and ready to climb. Since this is the Quantum Leap II—a level up from the solo Quantum Leap—I ask them to choose a climbing partner. I'm always fascinated by the expressions I see on their faces as they attempt to make their selection. Most try to find someone who does not appear scared; they're looking for someone who is both physically and emotionally stronger than they are. Also, typically, couples choose each other and most colleagues avoid one another—because of trust, or a lack thereof.

As I walk around the group to make sure they're safe and have a partner, I catch Peter trying to avoid Angela. *Why is Peter running from his wife?* I wonder. He's just about to ask someone else when an angry Angela grabs him by the arm:

"Hell no! You're coming with me!"

By now, both fear and excitement are hovering around the entire group. People are making jokes to hide their fears; others are just standing at their posts waiting for further instruction. When it's time for the couple to decide who goes first, Angela commands:

"You the man, you go!"

"Why don't you go, honey. I got your back." Peter responds.

"No, you go." She says.

"OK, I'll go, I guess I have no choice!" Peter shouts.

Peter charges toward the pole and begins his climb. He is about halfway—20 feet up—when he stops and yells:

"This will not be easy! You're not kidding, I can't stop shaking!"

A silent and terrified Angela is witnessing her husband's courage in action. It's then that I take the lead and share reassuring words to help Peter resume his climb:

"Take a few deep breaths! Take your time and continue when you're ready!"

He complies, returns to his focus, and climbs the rest of the pole.

"You're almost there! Good job, honey!" Angela joins in and exclaims.

As Peter prepares to squat and stand on the pole, he freezes:

"Oh my God, this is impossible! I can't control my body, I'm shaking like a leaf!"

I continue to help Peter with inspiring words. I also observe the change in Angela's face as she's rooting for her husband—it also looks as though she's feeling some remorse. Perhaps she's rediscovering some of Peter's attributes.

Peter gets his fear under control and is now standing on the pole's platform. Angela is preparing to join her husband up the 40-foot-high pole. But I can't help but notice something strange; she doesn't seem scared anymore. After being checked for safety, she goes straight to the pole, starts her ascent, and in less than two minutes is almost at the top, ready to stand next to her husband. It's tight up there and the real challenge is about to begin, as it's time to discover how strong their partnership really is. It's the role of the person standing on the pole to help their partner to join and stand with them, so they can unite as one and conquer both the pole and their fear. To be successful, this extraordinary bond requires courage, strength, determination, love, and compassion. Angela and Peter have to work things out between the two of them just like a team, even when they don't agree with one another.

There was no help from me or the group at that point; it was all coming from them. Angela and Peter were now inspiring and elevating each other—which is the core of every healthy relationship. We were witnessing the reawakening of a long-lost love and partnership. Peter reached out to Angela by holding her hand and slowly pulling her next to him. They were now standing harmoniously on top and gazing at the majestic view. Everyone had tears in their eyes as we witnessed the greatest act of love: unity. Their jump was the most beautiful I've seen. As they let go of each other, we could see and hear them scream their fears away. It was as soon as they'd touched the ground that they kissed each other for the longest 30 seconds, and then hugged everyone.

Shortly after their landing, I asked Angela and Peter if they could share with the group the three fears they'd written before their climb. Angela had written: fear of being alone, fear of losing my family, fear of dying. Peter's list was: fear of being alone, fear of losing my business, fear of losing my family.

It's astonishing to see the similarity between the two. This could explain why Peter was running from his wife and why Angela tried to control him like a helpless child.

For the rest of the program, Angela and Peter remained glued to each other. Like many, they may have had marital problems such as trust, control, and avoiding each other. All they had to do was take the courage to dig deep and reignite the flame.

With relationship issues, there are always two very different perceptions to a problem—what you see is not necessarily what I see—and taking time to share and understand those differences is important. Most give up way too quickly. They give up on themselves first, then on each other. It's no mystery that America is among the top three countries with the highest divorce rate. I know firsthand that making the choice to work through a relationship is hard work, but reviving the reasons we fell in love with each other the first time is well worth it. No matter the amount of problems you've accumulated along the years, you must find both strength and courage to clean up your emotional mess. Somewhere along the way you've buried your love for each other in a mountain of problems, and are just too emotionally tired to dig it out. Like I said before, it's easy to blame others for our own mistakes, so here's a fundamental truth for you: if you can see it in others, you have it in you!

Over the years I have found five issues that hold my clients back and obstruct their ability to live an inspired life: self-worth, trust, tranquility (the most neglected), their body, and a "desire to fight."

CHAPTER THREE

THE FIVE ISSUES

I know I can because I know I am!

LET ME FIRST start by defining the different issues facing us today. Issues that are interfering with our peace, confidence, sense of self-worth, etc. For most of my life, I believed I was a confident person. I knew what I wanted out of life and would work hard to get it. But confidence or self-esteem wasn't enough to buffer against fear or worry. What was missing was self-worth. I didn't value my life and potential.

Self-Worth

It has been a lifelong journey, but by reconnecting to my self-worth, I have been able to survive the ebbs and flows of life. To celebrate victories and see failures only as temporary and instructional. No challenge seems overwhelming or frightening. Whenever I have to make huge changes in my life, I don't shrink away; I know I can conquer it. A feeling of self-worth leads to freedom, because your mindset changes from "I'm not enough" to "I'm good enough."

There is a beautiful quote by my friend, writer and poet Suzy Kassem: "Before you were born and were still too tiny for the human eye to see, you won the race for life from among 250 million competitors. And yet, how fast you have forgotten your strength, when your very existence is proof of your greatness."

When you are at the mercy of others' approval, you are playing a dangerous game—the game of self-esteem—sometimes even putting your own health in harm's way just to fit the mold of society. As I mentioned earlier in this book, we live in a world that's fueled by the desire to impress others. When you discover self-worth—your ability to know who you are and what you want for yourself—you're no longer at the mercy of others' perception of who you should or shouldn't be, do or have. There is no need to impress or harm when you're connected to self-worth.

Self-worth makes you feel unique and unstoppable. It allows you to unleash the magic within, filling you, therefore, with unlimited energy and putting you on a path to reaching your aspirations, goals, and dreams. You can't fool yourself when it relates to self-worth. Sure, you can fake it by looking confident, but that goes to the wayside when you're confronted with your own behavior. Let me illustrate my point: If I think of myself as a good person, then do everything that suggests the opposite, I'm only fooling myself because deep down I know I'm not—so no sense of self-worth there. We have all seen the many disgraced individuals with immense power who exhibited huge confidence and so-called self-esteem for years but little to no self-worth. A person with self-worth is one who is inspired ; has self-care, self-compassion, and self-love. They have empathy; they love and respect others and can't do any harm, emotional, physical, or otherwise.

Trust

If you can't trust the universe, you end up being too cautious about the choices you make. There's a great French saying which I love and goes something like this: "When you throw a baby in the air, he laughs because he knows you will catch him. That's trust!" A baby believes its parent will step in and protect it. We should all be blessed with such a trusting mindset. With a trusting mindset, you will learn to walk through life without wasting energy on defending and protecting yourself against the world. The world won't seem like an unsafe place, full of dangers, pitfalls, and setbacks you cannot control or manage. A choice won't be a threat to your well-being. Instead, you will believe the choices offered to you will lead to a better life. A trusting mindset allows you the awareness that there are no so called "good" or "bad" choices, just what works or doesn't work. And even if the choices you make don't yield the desired outcome, you still can learn from them and move forward—hence, it's all good!

Tranquility

You need a sense of calm or tranquility to deal with life. But for most of us, we operate from a place of anxiety and fear. Anxiety and fear can distort reality. It can change the way we view situations and interactions with people. We add unnecessary meaning—which is usually negative—to the decision-making process. By doing so, it makes you see monsters where there are none. Furthermore, even if the monsters are small and manageable, you will make them bigger and scarier than they need to be (i.e., making a mountain out of a molehill). It also diminishes your ability to cope with the world. Anxiety will try to convince you that you can't do much, you can't feel emotions, you can't pursue your dreams. Similar to a distrustful mindset, you will see dangers in the world where none exist. Decision and choice making will be more about life preservation rather than about capturing your potential.

Body

It might seem weird to include the physical body here, but as a fitness and wellness coach I know how important it is to maintain health and well-being. If the mind and body aren't working well, it will be difficult to be present and have the energy to fight anxiety, fear, anger. The body should be a temple. It's the first defense against the world, so everyone needs to be aware of what they eat and drink, how much they sleep, etc. I encourage you to take care of yourself and be ready for anything the world will throw at you.

Desire to Fight

The best decisions are fueled by a desire to keep moving forward. We can get knocked down—and we will—but we need to have the energy to get back up and try again. I have worked with some very impressive people, including Oprah Winfrey, Barbra Streisand, and Sophia Loren. Of those three (in particular), their most common characteristics are taking risks and fearlessness. I will show that when offered decisions and choices to never *ever* shrink away from them. They are presented to you so you can prove yourself. Choices that are going to be difficult to make or might change your life are presented to you as a test. Get ready for them; it's what you need in your life to feel connected to the universe and your purpose. Learn to be a thriver and not just a survivor.

CHAPTER FOUR

SELF-WORTH

Look for love within.

PAUL THOUGHT THIS was a joke. He was loud, disruptive, and the previous night had gotten drunk during our communal dinner. As I saw him interact with his co-workers and other people at the retreat, it was clear he enjoyed being the class clown. He took it upon himself to deflate tense moments with a snicker or a whispered sassy comment. I kept my eye on him, and after our daily communal dinner asked him to stay back to chat. I knew he had a son, so we shared stories about how hard it is to raise children these days. As we were talking, I casually asked him, "Who are you, Paul?" He thought I was trying to put him in his place. I smiled. "Have you ever thought about who you really are? Not a dad, or a businessperson, but what your core is?"

"Ahhm. No, I guess I haven't."

A father, a husband, a salesman—he was trying to think of other terms to use. I pushed back. "Can you tell me a time when you were alone, tired, and ready to give up. Who were you then?"

He didn't understand. "When you were emotionally drained, not just financially, who were you?" We went back and forth like this for a while.

"So, this is my challenge to you: I want you to find out who you are."

As I got to know Paul over the weekend, he was someone you would look at and say, "He has everything. He has it figured out." But it was clear as day he wasn't happy and, sadly, probably didn't even know what happiness felt like. He was a zombie, completely empty on the inside and running after anything that looked like it had life. I see a lot of clients like this. They can pinpoint their progress in life with material objects:

"The car I bought with my first big sale."

"The vacation I went on after a great year at work."

The list goes on.

Their life has been curated around professional or material success, which is a sure sign it's a coping mechanism to cocoon themselves against emotions. For them, it's about chasing the feeling of elation while trying to avoid the letdown. Failure, real or perceived, is often painful, and they will do everything in their power to avoid it.

On the last day, Paul had taken my challenge seriously. He was self-aware enough to admit that he was a scared and fearful person. "At my core I'm angry," he confessed.

I was so proud of him. It takes strength and vulnerability to acknowledge your issues. It was a profound moment for him. Paul was like a lot of high achievers. They know how to work hard at all costs to get the corner office. They know how to struggle to achieve the impossible, pay bills, and have all the trappings of a successful person. But, deep inside, they are empty, frightened, and barely keeping their head above water. His role as the class clown was a way of connecting with people by being funny at the cost of others. I was like Paul once.

By the age of twenty-four, and as I mentioned earlier in this book, I was already a world champion bodybuilder and at the top of my game. I knew how to perform at the highest level, push my body to the limit, and was always ready for the next big fight . . . but all this was short-lived. Eventually my body, mind, and soul would completely fall out of alignment. Just like Paul, I had stopped engaging with myself and others. The problem was that Paul and I were motivated professionally, but stuck emotionally.

The zombie effect that Paul and I suffered from is all too common in today's society. I see it in my clients, my children, the cashier at the store, you name it. In our pursuit of perfection, we are spending a lot of time curating our selfie-ready persona. We have forced ourselves to live lives that are just for show—a lot of surface, but no depth. Someone may post inspirational quotes on their Instagram, but whether they believe it and live it is questionable. In her brilliant book *Daring Greatly*, Brené Brown succinctly explains the cause of the "zombie effect" as the "never enough" problem. We walk through life believing we are never enough. Never good enough. Never perfect enough. Never thin enough. The thinking goes something like this: if you aren't good enough to get into the right college, you aren't good enough for anything. If you aren't thin or fit enough, you aren't good enough to be loved. If you aren't good enough to be successful, you aren't good enough for much. This mentality that's constantly buzzing in our ears will only lead to disconnection from ourselves and others around us.

In some form or another, the "never enough" problem will lead to armoring. I've seen it happen. We make ourselves impervious to intense emotions, criticism, or failure. We harden ourselves against the realities of the world. The only thing we can focus on is us. Everything becomes about "me." We keep asking ourselves, am I enough, over and over again every day. When we find out we aren't enough, for whatever reason, we add another chink to our armor. With every addition we become fearful, distrustful, bitter, and unhappy. We slowly become a zombie; running after anything that has life and destroying ourselves in the process. Whether you are a CEO or a basement living, video game playing high school dropout, you aren't exempt from the zombie effect. None of us are exempt from it. I was living a successful life with a thriving business and happy family. Everything on the outside was fine, but, in my quest for perfection, I was cutting myself off from others. I was anxious, angry, physically drained, and consumed by fear and negativity. It has been a long journey— close to a decade—for me to find my life again.

What Does Self-Worth Mean?

"Do I have any value?"

"Am I useless?"

"Am I a good father?"

"What if I can't get this done?"

"I feel like I'm not very good at this job. Do I deserve this promotion?"

"He's cheating on me, I just know it."

"Am I not good enough to be loved?"

"Do I even matter?"

"I just can't handle these responsibilities."

These are some of the doubts and negative thoughts that swim through our heads every day. Clients have voiced them to me, and it always stings when I hear it. I know their potential and how much they can offer to the universe, but they want to believe all the negative noise. These narratives make them shrink when presented with a challenge and force them to stay in their comfort zone. Yes, force! Who in their right mind would want to believe these thoughts and let them affect their growth?

As human beings, we are trained to run away from pain, but what fascinates me is that my clients—and I'm sure a lot of you—run toward the pain caused by these negative thoughts or narratives. We choose to soak and wallow in the fear, the anxiety, and the shame rather than pushing forward. At some level, we are conditioned to believe the negative thoughts that have been fed to us. From my own personal experience, I know they can be deeply ingrained and hard to shake out of our system. At some level, Paul's narrative was that success was enough and believed he didn't deserve emotional connection. I keep coming back to these questions: Why believe you don't deserve emotional connection? Why believe promotions, success, and a new car isn't what you deserve? Why undermine your potential, emotionally, or otherwise?

I must admit that it isn't easy to eliminate these negative thoughts, as they result from many years of conditioning. But when you put in the effort to do so, you can finally experience freedom. Over the years, I have worked hard with my clients to eliminate these negative thoughts. While doing so, I have gotten a clearer picture of why we embrace and believe these negative thoughts, why we unconsciously want to be zombies living a lifeless existence filled with fear, resentment, and regret. It comes down to a lack of self-worth. Recently, I started seeing others using the term. Very few of us, though, have experienced true self-worth.

Forget even experiencing it, we actually don't have a definition for self-worth nailed down! I actually Googled the word hoping to find interesting articles or scientific papers, and to my complete surprise nothing came up. So, I sat down in my office, with a wonderful view of the Arizona desert, and forced myself to write down the definition. After a number of attempts, I couldn't approach the term straight on. Starting the sentence with "Self-worth means . . ." led nowhere. I didn't know how to finish the sentence. There were so many layers to the terms and pinning it all down felt like I was diminishing the power of self-worth. Instead, I took a different approach. I remembered the advice of one of my mentors, Dr. Dharma Singh Khalsa. When I told him that I was writing a book, he said, "Write from the heart."

I did exactly that and wrote the stories of my life and clients who took the journey to reclaim their self-worth. Looking at what I had I asked myself the following simple questions:

What are the common traits of people who possess and exhibit self-worth?

What does it feel like to experience self-worth?

When someone has self-worth, what are the choices they are able to make?

Armed with these questions, here's my definition of self-worth:

Self-worth is an undeniable and unshakable belief that you are worthy and valuable to your community, country, and the universe. It can never be taken from you, even if you willingly give it away. At your core, you are ready to be, to do, and comfortably live in and take advantage of the infinite number of choices offered to you every day. You live life from a place of knowing—a space where you trust yourself, the universe and can fearlessly take on challenges knowing your core won't be diminished if you experience failure.

Self-worth empowers you and transcends self-esteem. You expect change and embrace it, whether that might lead to unimaginable success or failure because, ultimately, you know how important it is to grow as a person. If you are living within a community, you don't feel small or big, but you know you belong. You are connected to others and can show compassion without feeling drained. Most importantly, self-worth is impervious to shame and humiliation.

As we look at the definition I have offered, it is easy to see that self-worth is an attitude. It is not only about believing in yourself. It really is about how you approach life, the opportunity it offers, and the people you will encounter. It can be broken down to the following affirmations:

I have worth and meaning regardless of my creed, sex, or nationality.
I seek self-validation.
I belong to the universe.
I can do anything.
I am fearless.
I know how to sense danger and to protect myself against it.
I will never look to sabotage myself.
I know what is in my best interest.
I know I'm good enough.
I know how to take criticism and change.
I know I need to grow and how to grow.

The simplicity of these affirmations might be surprising. Even so, you must be aware that it will take a lot of practice and patience to connect to your self-worth.

Infinity of Choices and Self-Worth

I am, first and foremost, a bodybuilder. A number of years ago, though, I toyed with the idea of taking up long-distance swimming in open waters. A bold decision, considering I live in Arizona. I started doing my research and looking at what I needed to do—both physically and emotionally—to start swimming. As I did my practice laps in the pool, my mind drifted to the concept of self-worth. That's when it dawned on me: swimming—especially in the open ocean—is a perfect metaphor for living life with self-worth.

Here's how it works: Let's say we all have to take a journey to cross the ocean so we can get to dry land. Like any athlete, you need to prepare for the swim. Some of us might be lucky and have great parents who provided us with all the tools necessary to complete the swim. But for the rest of us, we need to build up our skills before making the journey. This is often when people give up. It's extremely overwhelming to think of the vastness of the ocean and easy to become intimidated. Or, as All-American swimmer at Stanford University and open-water master swimming champion Alex Kostich says, to give into our fears and worries about encountering sharks and jellyfish, experiencing forces of nature and random acts of God. For anyone who isn't remotely ready, it will be very easy to believe that the journey is going to be dangerous and treacherous, and to listen to the negative thoughts encouraging you to stay near the beach, blame the universe, the people around us, and anything for our inability to make the journey.

Self-worth quiets the mental demons that will impede your swim. We will start the journey knowing that the universe will never actively work to deny us success. Even when there are sharks, jellyfish, nature, or random acts of God, the universe will provide us with resources and answers to our problems. It is our responsibility to look for and be receptive to them. Too often we like to play the helpless victim; the one who needs to be rescued from situations and/or circumstances out of our control. But the truth of the matter is we have the tools and resources to face any challenge. We always have the power to combat, live through, and solve any issues or crisis we may encounter. We never have to shrink away or stay in the shallows. With this attitude, we will become fearless.

The idea of sharks lurking deep in the water, looking for humans to eat, taps into our most primal fear. It doesn't help that the image of the shark from *Jaws* stalking, attacking, and murdering its victims is burned into our brains. The truth, though, is that sharks rarely attack humans. A lot of long-distance swimmers have been followed or visited by sharks on their trips but, alas, have never been eaten or attacked (they're just curious animals).

We all have sharks we worry about and obsess over and, sometimes, they can leave us terrified. My personal shark was a divorce. Your shark could be bankruptcy, the death of a loved one, a disease, you name it. I can tell you from personal experience that it will not kill you—unless you let it. My wife and I had built an amazing life together and had two beautiful children. I should have been happy, but I convinced myself that my wife couldn't love me. The negative thoughts flooded my brain. The next thing I knew my marriage was in tatters and I was heading toward divorce. I was exhausted. I couldn't keep swimming and wanted to drown. I thought it would be better to just let go and let the sea take me away. But my beautiful children helped me reconnect to my self-worth. I needed to keep living, growing, and evolving so I could be present for them. It took a lot of work, but I slowly reconnected to my self-worth.

Remember: self-worth can *never* be taken away from you. You might forget or give away your self-worth, but there's no such thing as a person who has no worth. As I connected to my own self-worth, I realized my divorce was a reminder to change course, to rethink my strategy in life. I also had to ask myself a very tough question: Was my behavior attracting sharks? Was I placing myself in situations that would inevitably lead to failure? While I pondered these tough questions, I kept swimming, learning, and changing for the better. My wife and I did get divorced, but we became best friends in the process. Our new family is healthy and happy again.

I hate jellyfish. I can't think of anyone who wants to encounter one when they are swimming. Unlike sharks, a jellyfish will sting and, I'm not going to lie, it will hurt. It can be hard, but a jellyfish sting is just a small setback. Is a co-worker making it difficult for you at work? Did you not get into the college of your dreams? Did you cheat on your diet again? Did you get laid off from your job?

Here's something I learned: in the excitement of the swim, you barely notice the sting of a jellyfish. Your adrenaline is pumping. You are focused on your goal, and actually forget that you've been stung by something out of a horror movie. Don't believe me? Listen to this amazing story Dwayne "The Rock" Johnson shared recently while he was in Vancouver, Canada:

> I was twenty-two years old, I came to this city for the first time. I was playing in the Canadian Football League, playing my first pro football game. I was playing for the Calgary Stampeders. We were playing the British Columbia Lions. I was so excited. Two days later, I got cut. Dreams shattered, sent home with seven bucks in my pocket. I was like, "Wait no, I gotta play in the NFL eventually. Those are my big goals. That's my dream."

Clearly the Rock had swum right into a swarm of jellyfish. He could have thrown up his hands and given up. Instead, he rethought what he wanted out of life. The NFL and CFL were the best things that didn't happen to him, he says.

Looking back at his experience, this is what he learned: "You gotta get up. You gotta have faith that the one thing you wanted to happen oftentimes is the best thing that never happened, so have faith and just keep that in mind and keep lugging away."

Shark attacks and jellyfish stings are just setbacks. They help you grow, evolve, and rethink your path and journey. Self-worth will remind you of this as you keep swimming. It will stop you from giving up and going back to the shallows. If you want to succeed and live life without regret, you need to keep yourself in the field of all possibilities and have access to an infinity of choices. As Dory, in *Finding Nemo*, always says: "Just keep swimming!"

Every successful swim needs an amazing crew that will offer emotional and tactical support while warning you when you are about to enter a dangerous situation. I have seen clients welcome anyone they know to join their crew. They will quickly learn, though, that an inadequate crew will lead to frustration, confusion, and failure. Trust me, I've been there! I was constantly confronted with uncaring parents, a school system that didn't want me to succeed, and an environment that was both physically and emotionally dangerous, I had no idea how to recruit a circle of adults who could support me. I was a loner. I did it on my own. I embarrassed myself and pushed for opportunities. It has taken me a lifetime to admit I needed help, and a lot of trial and error to find friends and mentors I could depend on. In the coming chapters, I will help you find the right type of people to circle yourself with.

With a purpose and a goal, self-worth is the fuel that allows you to pick only the best of the best to be on your crew. When you have value and worth as a person, you want only the best people to surround you. My crew has helped me navigate rough waters, cheered me on as I swam against the current, and told me over and over again that I could do it. I trusted and believed them. Soon, I knew in my heart I could do anything.

When I approach my clients armed with my definition of self-worth and my analogy to back it up, they are at first apprehensive, then defensive. It's hard for many of them to wrap their heads around it. They are taught by therapists and doctors that they have to outthink their negative thoughts and intellectually force themselves to take the leap or swim out into open waters. So, understandably, they are expecting lengthy sessions during which they mine their psyche, past, and try to rectify the hurt caused to them. The belief is that the past is what's holding us all back. It's true to some degree, and it can be powerful when it's brought back to be compared with current life situation, feelings, and emotions. Past and present are then fused together to create understanding. The negative thoughts/narratives are rooted in our past, but the issues and problems occur in the present. We are affected everyday by these unnecessary thoughts. They stop us from functioning and thriving in our daily lives. Even if the mental demons live in the past, they are alive and well in the present. We need to attack them now. But my clients understandably have asked the question, *What does self-worth and swimming, have to do with this? How can I take the leap, swim out into open waters, erase my negative thoughts, and overcome my mental demons with self-worth?*

By affirming your self-worth, you are connecting to a powerful life force that won't run out or dry up. From now until the end of time, you are and will be worthy and valuable to the universe, your community, and the people around you—there's no beginning or end to your worth. You will start believing that you are more than the image society has offered you or that you have created for yourself. You're more than just a parent or the college degree you have or don't have.

Negative thoughts/narratives might persist and clog your brain, but it will be replaced by a voice that says, "You are valuable. You deserve more." Powerful statements that will drown out and unshackle you from paralysis and fear. As I started to meditate on my self-worth, my thinking pattern changed from "I can't" to "I deserve to." I felt an inner forward motion that fueled and propelled me into action and growth. I knew I deserved the opportunities and even the challenges I was going to face. I was eager to leave the shallows and take a leap into the unknown.

Our power as humans comes from taking our destiny into our own hands. By connecting to self-worth, you are assuring yourself access to the field of all possibilities. As you swim out to the open ocean and encounter sharks, jellyfish, and random acts of God, self-worth will guide and keep whispering, "Yes, you are worth the tough journey," "Yes, you are valuable and important enough to enjoy success."

Self-Worth vs. Self-Esteem

1. On the whole I am satisfied with myself.
2. At times I think that I am no good at all.
3. I feel I have a number of good qualities.
4. I am able to do things as well as most other people.
5. I feel I do not have much to be proud of.
6. I certainly feel useless at times.
7. I feel that I am a person of worth, at least the equal of others.
8. I wish I could have more respect for myself.
9. All in all, I am inclined to feel that I am a failure.
10. I take a positive attitude toward myself.

These questions are part of the test created by Morris Rosenberg and is the most popular self-esteem questionnaire still being used. Most of my clients do really well on it; their self-esteem is pretty high. Their answers show self-confidence and self-regard. It's long been believed that self-esteem is a good marker of a well-adjusted human being. We know just anecdotally that can't be right. I know plenty of clients, friends, and family who have very positive views of themselves, yet put themselves in very self-destructive situations.

I mentioned in chapter one that, as a society, we put a lot of importance on self-esteem and self-confidence. We obsess over our children being confident enough to survive the rough and tumble real world. The advice I used to get often was "Fake it till you make it"; fake your confidence and you will start believing in yourself. It was the worst advice I had ever received. Faking it just made me feel like an imposter. I agree with psychology professor Kristin Neff's assessment: our obsession with self-confidence in our culture is misguided and pointless. Her argument is simple: self-esteem and narcissism go hand in hand. In our pursuit for self-esteem, we constantly push ourselves to be better, to be special, and to be one of a kind, so we puff ourselves up. The social media culture is a great example. The more followers and likes you get, the more social cachet you have. The content of your character isn't important anymore. As long as you take pictures of yourself next to a mansion, at the exclusive resort or club, and post them, you can expect your self-esteem to grow with your likes, retweets, and comments. Deep inside, though, we are still empty. The first sign of failure or a challenge, self-esteem flees and leaves us with fresh opportunities for deception that most find difficult to grapple with. Our aspirations, our desires, our dreams, our successes are all for show; there's nothing sustaining our souls.

Researchers are concerned about the role self-esteem plays in maintaining social hierarchy. It is very human to compare ourselves to others, and research has found two ways we do this: upward and downward. We look up to people and hope to be like them; "I want to be as skinny as her," "I wish I was wealthy and as smart as him." Once again reinforcing the idea of "not good enough." Downward comparison means looking down at someone who we perceive to be lesser than. We look down on the nerdy kid in school or the co-worker who never gets their work done on time, just so we can feel better about ourselves. We experience it every day on social media; people calling each other names, fat shaming, trolling just to make themselves feel smarter or prettier. Regardless of the type of comparisons we take part in, both are extremely unhealthy.

A confident person can be very obtuse and sees a skewed version of the world. Having self-esteem can obstruct your ability to take responsibility for your bad habits or behavior and actually, work on changing them. Sometimes even denying their existence. My favorite example for this was when assemblyman John Vasconcellos set up the "California Task Force to Promote Self-Esteem and Personal and Social Responsibility" in 1986. Vasconcellos believed that if he could raise his constituent's self-esteem, he could put a dent in various social ills. Higher self-esteem would mean no more drug dealers, teen pregnancy, violent crime, arson. You guessed right: it didn't work. Drug dealers still thrived. Teenagers got pregnant.

This might seem like a misguided story. Emerge, a domestic violence prevention program run by psychologist David Adams, whose clients were mostly abusive men, shares a frightening story:

> I once did an intake on a batterer who had been in psychotherapy for three years, and his violence wasn't getting any better. I said to him, "Why do you think you hit your wife?" He said to me, "My therapist told me it's because I don't feel good about myself inside."

For this man, going to therapy and meditating on his self-esteem didn't promote change. He still abused his wife and it didn't seem like he had any idea why he continued his violent actions. Change can only occur when we experience self-awareness and actually work on becoming better people, regardless of one's needs for counseling.

I get asked a lot, why self-worth? It's because self-esteem doesn't allow us to be imperfect human beings who need to change and grow. If we want to take hold of our destiny and live in the field of possibilities, we need to embrace change and the growth process. Self-worth will allow you to do just that. When we see each other as imperfect humans who are all working hard to become better, it will help us become kinder and nicer people. Our immediate instinct needs to switch from bullying and demeaning to forgiveness and compassion. We all belong to the universe. It's our responsibility to take care of each other.

Cultivating Self-Worth Skills

When my clients and I sit down to reconnect to their self-worth, it's a very intense session. I ask them to surrender to their past. What I tell my clients is this: the hurt, the humiliation, the pain, and the anger has to be surrendered. If not, it will weigh you down and keep you in the shallows. The past can never be rectified. This doesn't mean you ignore it or forget it, but instead learn to become an observer of the past. View it without judgement or engagement. Your access to the field of possibilities and infinite choices can only occur in the present and future. By only looking back, you miss out on the now.

Next, I encourage them to acknowledge their present state; they are broken, happy, sad, or all the above. We work on understanding that their self-worth is intact and alive within them. It's a life force that's breathing and can fuel their growth.

Part of acknowledging your present is to look within. When I asked Paul who he really was, I was asking an ancient Vedic question. In the Vedic tradition, when yogis are in pursuit of their true self, they start by saying, "I'm not this and I'm not that." The Sanskrit term for this is *Neti, Neti*. I ask my clients to do the same. They have to slowly unravel what holds them together and get to their core—their life force. I ask them to slowly unwrap their identity: "I'm not a mom. I'm not a daughter. I'm not the best pianist at high school." As you do this, you are searching for your life force, your passion, your dreams, your fears and your true self.

Here's my *Neti, Neti* exercise:

Deep breathing (3 minutes)
Ask who you aren't. Write the answers down.
Do this every day until you get to your core.

Some of the answers I have seen are:

I'm not a victim.

I'm not a bully.

I'm not an angry person.

I'm not just a mother.

I'm not fat.

I'm not insignificant.

I'm not stupid.

I don't want you to be fooled by the simplicity of this exercise, as it can take months to peel back the layers and push fears to the surface to discover your self-worth. Others have asked, what if the answers are all negatives? The core of a human being, their self-worth, can only be positive. If you want to find it and acknowledge it, you have to look for the positive within yourself.

One of my clients, James, after doing this exercise, realized he was unhappy and confused. He was a lost little boy. It was a tremendous breakthrough. Now, he needed to find the life force, the positive, within himself. After a lot of soul searching, he came to see me and said with defiance, "I'm not my father." If he wasn't his father, he didn't have to be a doctor and live in fear. It was all clear to him. He gave up his career and became a schoolteacher. Teaching was his passion, and with that as his foundation he was able to face his fear and trust in himself. By admitting who he wasn't, James could reclaim his worth and fight for who he was and what he wanted out of life. He was ready to take the leap.

Jumping into the field of possibilities can be quite difficult, yet immensely liberating. Taking the leap is admitting and affirming your power to change your thinking pattern and taking action of your life. The only way to be fully human is to express your power of choice.

The next step for cultivating self-worth is to choose and affirm your core values. If you aren't living a value-driven life, it will be hard to have a meaningful, fulfilling life and find freedom from what's holding you back. In retrospect, what were the core values that sustained me through happiness and tragedy? Hard work, commitment, kindness, balance, and love. These are the core values that have kept me going when I faced sharks, jellyfish, and random acts of God. When I ask my clients, who are you? I'm also asking them what core values sustain and give them meaning in their life.

Write out your core values on a piece a paper and keep it on you for a whole month to remind you to live a value driven and worthy life each day. After the first month, write down any changes you have experienced. I encourage my clients to do this on a monthly basis. It's the only and best way to be actively part of constructing meaning and living a worthy life. Obviously, there are many personal and professional core values you can identify with, but for the sake of this exercise just pick a couple and come back to them often.

Here Are My Top 10 Core Values:

1. Love
2. Strength
3. Compassion
4. Hard work
5. Perseverance
6. Commitment
7. Kindness
8. Balance
9. Forgiveness
10. Authenticity

Three Steps to Your *Neti, Neti* and Core Values

The following three-step exercise is a powerful and effective tool to connecting to self-worth and avoiding conflicts.

Step 1: Do your *Neti, Neti* exercise until you identify and connect to who you truly are. Refer to the exercise above.

Step 2: Write out your core values on a piece of paper and keep it on you for a whole month to remind you to live a value driven and worthy life every day.

Step 3: If and when you feel disconnected from your self-worth, match your core values with your emotions.

Matching Your Emotions with Your Core Values: Diffusing Conflict

Unmanaged stress, fear, anxiety, doubt, lack of sleep, and hunger—to name just a few—can be triggers to experiencing a conflict between your emotions and your core values, or between your mind and your soul. When that happens, you just need to step back from whatever is creating the conflict, clear your mind, surrender to the present moment, and reconnect the two so you can be true to yourself and your commitment to your core values. But how do you know when you've entered a conflict? When your emotions have taken ahold of your peace. When you delve straight into the problem with absolutely no evidence or fact supporting what you perceive. When that happens, you become part of the problem and you create inner conflict. To illustrate, I want to share a real event that took place a few years ago.

Michelle is the founder and CEO of a midsize company in a large, metropolitan city. She hired me to help her and her team of top executives with their overall physical, mental, and emotional fitness. Michelle had a specific goal in mind: to create a new and healthier wellness environment within her company. She was concerned about the health and well-being of four of her top producers, whom were also at high risk for corporate burnout—now a legitimate diagnosis classified by the World Health Organization (WHO). This is what I do; I help high-performance, high-productivity individuals avoid physical and emotional chaos via fitness and wellness. But there was a slight problem: she needed me in Chicago the very next week, and my schedule was already booked solid. "I heard some great things about you and the way your work with people, we need you Nordine! Please make it happen," she asked. So I made a few calls to reorganize my schedule.

I arrived Sunday evening on time for a briefing dinner at a local hotel. Michelle and her husband, Victor, were waiting at the lobby. Upon sitting at our table at the hotel's restaurant, I felt both a mixture of anxiety and excitement emanating from Michelle. "I have something to share with you, Nordine. We have a logistical problem."

"Oh yeah? And what's that?" I replied.

"Our company is being acquired by huge multinational and my team and I are involved in the negotiations. The talks are taking place during the same time as your program, in adjacent meeting rooms. I am not sure how we're going to do that. I'm sorry!" She continued with an apologetic tone.

"That could present a little problem," I whispered.

"I am so sorry! Do you want to cancel? We would still pay your fee," she said.

Committed to perform my job, I replied: "I'm here Michelle, let's do this!"

The rest of the dinner went with no other surprises. She felt a lot better, and we talked about the logistics of our weeklong program, which began the next day at 9 a.m. As you can imagine, and under such circumstances, the atmosphere felt very tense. Sitting around a huge meeting table were five anxious individuals: Amy, John, Peter, Will, Pam, and Michelle. As I entered the room, and based on their rather loud discussion, their attention wasn't focused on me, but rather on the acquisition.

This will be a long program I thought to myself. To bring the energy up, I told a cute story about how my little French bulldog would play tricks by stealing my clothes and making me run half naked around my kitchen island. They all burst into laughter. I had gotten their attention, and we began the program.

Michelle wasn't kidding; the negotiations were taking place in the very next room. The whole program was about regaining inner peace and eliminating unnecessary stress, yet these people were going to be engaged in serious negotiations. It wasn't going to be easy.

The first three days were hard for all of us. Unorthodox, you could say, but imagine alternating wellness sessions with highly stressful corporate negotiations, one after the other, for three consecutive days; learning about managing stress at 9 a.m. then practicing next door with real-life corporate wolves at 10:30 a.m. Or working out at 2 p.m. and returning to the negotiation table at 3:30 p.m.—our sessions were 90 minutes—followed by their hour-long negotiation meetings. I'd never experienced something like this before or since. Total chaotic mess is how one would describe this event. But what if I told you it was a perfect and synergetic experience—somehow, one situation would help another. When there was tension or disagreement in one room, there was calm and enthusiasm in the other. A method learned in one room helped diffuse a conflict in the other. It worked out perfectly. The team was instantly putting to practice what they'd learned and were experiencing immediate results.

But the biggest take away of this experience was when they all had to learn and apply their *Neti, Neti* and core values exercises. During the negotiations, there were many attempts to intimidate and lure them into corporate traps. Sometimes, they threw some disrespectful and derogatory tones at Michelle and her team, thus triggering an avalanche of negative thoughts and sending some of them into a reactive mode. But each occasion, they could control themselves and come back while maintaining total integrity to their self-worth. Because they were taking in fresh content, they could engage in real term and avert any negativity. They'd learned how to diffuse external conflicts using their core values. Although everyone had experienced some kind of challenge during the negotiations and could diffuse them, I want to use Michelle as an example for this book's purpose. When faced with a particular incident that took place during the talks, here is what helped her.

Michelle's *Neti, Neti* exercise:
(Done during the program)

Deep breathing (3 minutes)

I'm not just a boss.

I'm not just a mother.

I'm not just a wife.

I'm not a bad person.

I'm not naive.

I'm not fat.

I am a strong and intelligent woman.

Michelle's list of core values:
(Done during the program)

Strength	Intelligence
Love	Confidence
Kindness	Calm
Courage	Focus
Compassion	Assertive

Michelle's diffusing conflict exercise:
(Performed while taking a bathroom break
immediately after the incident's occurrence)

"Michelle feels *humiliated* when *one of the lawyers attempts to question her loyalty.*"

Her emotion is: *humiliated.*

Her core value is: *strength.*

Does her emotion match her core value? *No.*

As you can see, Michelle's emotion wasn't matching her core value. However, she was being proactive by responding positively and reminding herself that she is a *strong* person who wouldn't allow anyone to humiliate and disrespect her; remember that *strength* was one of her core values. Because she had her list and she was taking the time to remind herself of who she was and what her cores values were, she could instantly use her *strength* to climb back up to her self-worth and diffuse the conflict. It only takes a few deep breaths to get back to the present moment and make that connection. Total time spent: three minutes. This could've turned into a disaster if it weren't for Michelle's desire to fight back with strength, calm, and confidence—three of her core values.

Now that you know how it works, use this exercise the next time you feel disconnected or in conflict with your core values.

Like Michelle and her team, I invite you to do your *Neti, Neti* exercise and create your list. Remember that it's not what happens to you that matters, but how you respond to what happens to you that does. This exercise will help you connect and maintain them. Write your emotions and match them with your core values. Are they congruent or in conflict with one another?

Your turn:

"I feel _____ when _____."

My emotion is: _____.

My core value is: _____.

Does my emotion match my core value? _____.

CHAPTER FIVE

TRUST

Let go . . .

IT WAS AN unusually cold night in Albuquerque, New Mexico. I was wearing every piece of clothing I had, but I still felt the chill in my car. To be fair, when I was packing to come to America, I wasn't planning on being homeless. Since I was little and living in our small apartment in northern France, MTV, John Wayne, and hamburgers all seemed so wonderful and novel. It was my dream to travel and live in the United States—the land of the free and home of the brave. When my former mentor and coach Serge Nubret—a.k.a. "The Black Panther," a five-time Mr. World and Mr. Universe, runner-up Mr. Olympia after Arnold Schwarzenegger—offered me a once-in-a-lifetime opportunity to work in New Mexico, I jumped at the chance. I was promised a great salary, a room in his house, and a chance to apply for a green card. My first trip to America started with so much hope, but then fate stepped in.

I was about to start a new life. I was smart enough to know I would need to work hard and that the streets weren't going to be paved with gold, but I wasn't ready for what was going to happen next. Serge had partnered up at a gym and we were working for him. We had plenty of new equipment and there was buzz around the place. The word was out that there were two world-class coaches in one city—let alone in one gym—and do I need to tell you that it was packed every day? It was so packed that it was nearly impossible to take care of everyone.

People wanted to work out with us, to be coached by us. Some less fortunate who couldn't afford to pay for the training sessions would show up at the door even before we opened just to get a "Mr. Universe" signed autograph. It was both overwhelming and exalting.

But by the end of the month, when we were supposed to get a paycheck, Serge was evasive. He had promised me if I talked up his business, he would pay me and, as I mentioned, even help me get a green card. I didn't want to offend him, so I kept quiet and worked my hardest. At the end of the second month, I still hadn't been paid. I started to get desperate. I asked one of my co-workers if he had gotten a paycheck. Bad move. Serge heard about it and next thing I knew he told me I wasn't welcome in his house anymore, and I was fired. Just like that! Five thousand miles away from home!

I was heartbroken. Serge was my mentor, I've known him since 1984, long before I came here. He had helped me conquer the world of bodybuilding and nurtured my talents. He was like a father to me. I felt like the rug had been pulled from beneath me. This is how I ended up with only three hundred dollars to my name, shivering in my rental car, wearing all the clothes I had to keep warm.

For three days, while sitting in my car and watching Americans go about their everyday life, I really hoped for a future here. I could no long envision my dream coming true. I was so close, but I had to admit I couldn't do it this time. I was mentally and emotionally drained; I had no energy left to get excited about anything. I had disconnected from my self-worth. After arguing with myself for a couple of days, I made the difficult decision to move back to France. As a final gesture, I wanted to buy a souvenir for my mother. She was the one who had pushed me hard to pursue my dreams. When I was a kid, she would take me to the library and we would flip through American magazines and history books. When we got a TV, she would watch *Dynasty* and *The Bold and the Beautiful*. Her image of the USA was of glamorous men and women living very complicated love lives.

I found a jewelry store in a strip mall where I thought I could buy something affordable. I walked around in the store looking for something cheap, yet expensive looking. My mother would love to wear a gaudy piece of jewelry and show it off to her friends. The yellow-gold bracelets were very pretty. The store clerk came by and asked if I wanted to see anything. I nodded and pointed to one intricate-looking bracelet. As he handed it to me, he stared a little too hard. I asked how much it was and he stared a little longer at me. I realized it was because of my thick French accent. I apologized and slowly repeated my question. Instead of answering me, he asked, "Are you Nordine, the bodybuilder, Mr. Universe?" I was stunned into silence for a second. "Yes. Yes, I am."

"I heard rumors that you were in town, but I didn't want to believe it! So it's true! I used to have you on a calendar on my bedroom wall. Wow, you were great. Hi, I'm Ahmad. Why are you here?"

There were two stories I could tell this kid: his hero was homeless and had failed at trying to make a life in America or tell him I was here on a business trip—thinking of starting a new gym right here in Albuquerque—so I could say. I still remember this. I took a deep breath and let out a sigh. It was a moment of reckoning. Was I going to live a lie? I had my pride. How could I share my situation with a kid who idolized me? I imagined how his face would switch from amazement to disgust. Finally, it came down to me realizing I didn't have anything to lose. At that moment, I was homeless with not much to my name. I couldn't outlive the truth. I sheepishly told him I was living in my car. Before I knew it, I was spilling my whole story to him. To my surprise, he didn't miss a beat; he immediately made a call and offered to share a bedroom at his best friend's apartment.

So there I was, living with three young guys! They all offered to give up their room for me and gladly sleep on the couch. Perks of fame? It was a stroke of fate I couldn't imagine. Ahmad, whose father was an important and well-known businessman, also was a law student and when he heard I was trying to make my life in America suggested a meeting with an immigration lawyer. The following week I had a meeting where we went through my options. The lawyer went through the list:

Are you a doctor or a scientist? Nope.

Do you have an American girlfriend who you could marry? Nope.

Do you have a million dollars in the bank? Nope.

Are you a refugee? Nope.

Do you have a family member who is an American citizen who could sponsor you? Nope.

Can an employer sponsor you? Nope.

Have you won any type of award? Yes, I was Mr. Europe, Mr. World, and Mr. Universe.

This is how I ended up applying for and receiving a green card under the category of "Alien of Extraordinary Ability." Even today, only a few people have received a green card through this category. The list of people who have are pretty impressive: John Lennon, Monica Seles, Piers Morgan, Justin Bieber. It was not lost on me how amazing and miraculous my journey had been. From being homeless with no prospects to a green card holder who could take on every opportunity offered to him and start building my all-American life. I became a trainer for a gym and after I had found my way around and my English got better; I started my personal training business. The Maloof brothers, the former owners of Sacramento Kings and hoteliers, were my first clients. People like Jim and John Thomas, a.k.a. "The Salsa Twins," followed suit within weeks. In just a year, I had completely transformed my life.

I've mentioned it earlier in this book, and I'm mentioning it again in this chapter, because to describe trust, there's no more powerful than this: "When you throw a baby in the air, they laugh because they know you will catch them." What if, like the baby, you kept trusting as you traveled through the ups and downs of this journey called life? Not so easy, you'd say! It's hard to trust when you get hit so many times. But who exactly does the hitting? It's you! Yes, you! You do the hitting because somehow, along the way, you stop trusting and start doubting—you lose faith in yourself.

Doubt, my friend, is a very nasty emotion, and can kill all hopes for success. The child within is always there, always trusting. We should always remember that we are blessed with a trusting mindset. With this simple awareness, you can walk through life without wasting energy protecting yourself against opportunities. Instead of cowering from what life offers, you can embrace it.

How do you achieve a trustful mindset? You need to believe in your instincts.

Nature and the universe have given you gut instincts to protect you from the dangers of the world. You need to teach yourself and practice listening to them. Most importantly, everyone has a story, a journey, or narrative, and it's very important to believe in it. Even when I was homeless, I trusted in my journey. I knew my dreams and hard work would be rewarded. Despite my self-resignation to leave America, I just had to let my journey play out.

It's important to trust yourself and create a trustful mindset. In order to maintain trust, you need to feel comfortable being vulnerable. Throughout my life I have put myself in uncomfortable and vulnerable situations. It was humiliating at times, but I needed to trust my narrative and believe that the universe would help me reach my goal. We should also be reminded that the opposite of trust—distrustfulness—can lead to bitterness, resentfulness, and can destroy every aspect of your life. It will not only paralyze decision making and stop one from entering the field of possibilities, but can make them cling to the idea that the world is a dangerous and frightening place, out to destroy their dreams and self-worth.

————

Why do most of my clients experience a huge lack of trust once they arrive at the top of the pole, and hesitate before jumping? After all, they've accomplished the most important part of the climb, right? Wrong! Trust is lost when fear sets in. Even when they are supported by the climbing harness and are safely belayed by trained professionals, they still don't trust. This phenomenon is a common theme among most people, and especially among high achievers. If you don't believe me, ask the billionaire who sits at the top of an empire. They work hard to climb the ladder of success; they experience fear, defeats, humiliation, and sometimes even tragedy, but they finally get to the top. And once up there, it can feel terrifying and very lonely. They feel alone, surrounded by the hugeness of the empire they've created. You have hundreds or perhaps thousands of people working for you but you want to control everything. You feel that everyone wants a piece of you, and you want to protect yourself—you become saturated with mistrust. You won't allow yourself to feel vulnerable, to be yourself! Can it be from the fear of losing it all? What's the climber at the top of the pole afraid of? Dying? We could say that, ultimately, this would be the right answer. But what's beneath the fear of death? I'll tell you, it's is the fear of being vulnerable; it's what leads us to be distrustful.

During the particularly hot summer of 2003, I was sitting in my office at the Body Mindfulness Center at Miraval, engrossed in preparing a presentation I was to give at the LA Sports Club in Beverly Hills. Suddenly, from out of nowhere, a very frustrated guest that I did not know, covered in sweat, burst into my office.

"I don't understand, I'm totally confused!" he exclaimed. "There are too many things to do in here. I can't possibly do them all; I'd kill myself! This is way too much!"

"Sir, please just calm down, take a deep breath, and have a seat," I replied. I went on to explain that his experience at Miraval was about awareness, trusting, and choice—a choice that must come from the heart, not from logic or even wanting. "You don't have to do everything. Your life is here in the now so just be and let things come to you. Let them choose you," I told him. "You'll know what to do then."

"OK. I'm Gary by the way," he said with a much calmer but still skeptical tone, "I'll give it a try."

During that stay, I only saw Gary twice—once during a class I was teaching and once a week later, right before his departure. Again, with no hesitation, he interrupted what I was doing (I was in the middle of a session with no other than the amazing Barbra Streisand). This time, I really was taken aback—not because of the interruption, but because Gary not only looked like he'd changed physically, but looked different energetically. He looked completely renewed. "I had to come share my info and thank you as I'm leaving today," Gary said. "I must tell you that I feel both sadness and happiness."

I didn't quite understand, so I asked, "I'm sorry, sadness? Why sadness?" I could see an intrigued Ms. Streisand out of the corner of my eye.

"I am sad to leave this amazing place, but I'm also happy because I met someone," he revealed.

"Someone? That's great! May I know who's that lucky person?" I asked.

"Yes, it's me!" He shot back with a smile that told it all. My eyes began to well with tears, and so did Gary's (and Ms. Streisand's). It was awe-inspiring. Gary had finally reconnected with himself—a self he'd never truly known before. We then hugged each other and said goodbye.

You can only imagine how this experience would leave Barbra and I marveling about Gary's newly discovered self. Although I've had many similar experiences with guests before, this one caught both my attention and curiosity. I needed to know what triggered Gary's speedy transformation; how he transcended his negative emotions—from angry and doubtful to calm and mindful—and created a renewed self. What did he mean when he said that he'd met himself? What was going on in his head and in his heart?

With a heightened curiosity, I called Gary the next morning to find out what activities he'd partaken in and who said what to him. Something or someone had to trigger the one or more things that helped him make such a shift. In the past, I had guests tell me it was a combination of the people's energy and the resort's serenity that would facilitate the shift. But in Gary's case—and as I came to discover—it was far more than that.

I don't recall the entire phone conversation, as this happened almost 20 years ago. But the following part of the call remains cemented in my brain and has been instrumental to both my personal growth and my ability to understand my clients better; it helped lay the foundation for my future career as a health and wellness coach.

When prompted with the question "What triggered the shift?" Gary's answer was loud and clear: "You did!"

"Me? Why me?"

"Yes, you," He continued. "That day when I came to your office, I was furious and confused. But something about your ability to calm me down and your willingness to take the energy and share inspiring and guiding wisdom. In just a few minutes, you gave me the tools to navigate my way in a sanctuary filled with soothing and almost overwhelming energy—an energy I never knew before. You see, Nordine, for most of my life I always knew how to work hard, always on the run and always after the next business deal. Go, go, go was my dad's motto—he taught me hard work and tough love, so following my heart was novel to me."

"I can understand, it must have been difficult." I said.

"Yes, at first it was! I had to force myself not to get tempted by the urge to take several fitness classes in a row. Distress with more stress, I guess. The do, do, do concept of modern society—sadly a concept I was much too familiar with. In the past, when you signed up for a fitness retreat, they taught you to take class after class, activity after activity—nonstop. Your idea of "trust and choice" was very appealing and I wanted to try it. Besides, who wouldn't want to follow Mr. Universe's advice, right? So I thank you, Nordine."

"It was my pleasure, Gary. Can you take me through the process that helped you transcend your old self?"

"After I left your office, it was like going on a roller-coaster ride in my head. I was battling my emotions: anger, frustration, doubt, etc. I had a super hard time trusting myself, but as I walked the premises and stumbled upon the tranquility, serenity, calm, and more calm, it permeated my being and I began letting go of the stuff. I started listening to my heart instead—just as you suggested—taking a meditation class here and a yoga class there, signing up for the equine experience, and just feeling the energy from everyone I met, both from other guests and staff alike. As I was slowly drifting into peacefulness, my mind began to peel off the layers; I was getting to the core of my being. I let it all go. I took out my mental trash—years of it! I remembered your commending yet soothing voice saying: *Just trust and let go*. And I did! Eventually, I felt a complete shift just a couple of days before my departure. And I must be honest with you, Nordine. The hardest part was departure day. But I learned so much and I let go of so much more. Again, thank you."

"Wow, this is amazing, Gary. Thank you. You're the one who did the work. I just helped facilitate the process. I am just glad that you knew how to use the tools we gave you. I have one more question for you. Since you left, how did your experience help you in your everyday life, if at all?"

"Are you kidding me?" Gary exclaimed. "Those tools saved my life; my business, my marriage, and my relationship with my kids. Before my trip I was an angry and distrustful person, always micromanaging people—a complete control freak! I had no time for others—not even for myself—and had no personal life to speak of. I lived in my head mostly, and when it came to taking care of myself, my health and well-being, I stirred away from even seeing a doctor, as I was afraid he'd tell me to slow down or afraid to find out I was burning the candle at both ends. For years I climbed the ladder of success, using sheer willpower and hard work, forgetting about how it felt to just be. Success had a whole different meaning then. Yesterday, I was an unhappy successful man; today I'm happy and even more successful. I wake up every day with energy, vitality, and passion, and I share all that with everyone who crosses my path. So yes, the tools I learned from you helped by allowing me to let go of the stuff that had already let go of me, the stuff that was no longer serving me. It allowed me to return to sanity." Gary and I concluded the call by wishing each other well. We still are in contact, and he still visits.

As Gary eloquently said, "When you trust the universe, you slowly return to sanity." The walls you've built to shield yourself from the rest of the world crumble and you experience clarity. Trusting will restore your innate ability to create and manifest your deepest desires.

In Gary's case, it was a combination of energies—the people and the landscape's—that allowed him to transcend his ego and make the shift. But the same can happen to anyone, anywhere. Just let go! In the next chapter, you'll discover how to use calm to gain mental and emotional strength.

CHAPTER SIX

TRANQUILITY

Calmness leads to strength.

I WAS BARELY nineteen, and this was my first competition. I walked down the dimly lit hallway to the brightly lit stage. There were impressive athletes waiting to go on stage and prove they deserved to be given a chance to advance to the semifinals of the Mr. Belgium competition. As I looked at them waiting for their time under the spotlight, I took a deep breath and brought the focus to my heart. As I walked up the stairs, I turned to the audience, gave them a practiced big smile, and began my routine: flex my quads, bend my knees slightly, puff out my chest. Then I went blank. I started sweating. I couldn't remember the rest of my routine. For the next three excruciating minutes I just kept repeating my first two moves. The music finally stopped, and I walked off the stage, shaking. The audience was booing and laughing. I was so embarrassed I couldn't make eye contact with anyone. "What happened?" my coach asked. I couldn't even give him an answer. My mouth was dry and I could feel the back of my throat burning.

Just a week before, when my coach, Michel, asked me to be part of the team for this competition, I couldn't believe it. *He's finally acknowledging my talents*, I thought. I spent the entire week watching my teammates in the gym and teaching myself a routine. This was the moment to show my coach and everyone who had seen me in the gym that I had talent. All of my hard work meant something. When I told my mother, she didn't quite understand why I was so happy. Bodybuilding was new to her, but she wanted me to succeed and so made me a sandwich right before the tournament and wished me good luck. I didn't tell my father, who wasn't convinced that spending time in the gym would benefit me. We were an immigrant family and he couldn't quite understand the trend. He wanted me to go to college and become an accountant. To prove him wrong, I imagined winning a trophy at the contest and showing it to him. *See, I have the ability and I can be successful as a bodybuilder.*

I was sitting in the locker room after the event, completely shell shocked. Everyone walked by, and while some were kind enough to give me a pat on the back, others avoided me, worried my bad luck would rub off on them. I was fighting back tears and trying to figure out where and how it had all gone wrong. My dreams of fame similar to Arnold Schwarzenegger seemed shattered. How was I going to go home and tell my mom I didn't win the trophy? I had wanted to win so badly, but I let my anxiety and fear overtake me. It was a devastating blow to my confidence. I can still see my young self, hunched over, freaked out about my future.

When the universe presents you with a choice, or decision, or opportunity, you need to be ready to take it. Anxiety, fear, and obsessive thinking will limit your decision-making ability. It will say, "you can't do this," "you can't love or be loved," "you can't pursue your dreams"—don't even try. When we experience anxiety, we sometimes forget that it is just a symptom of the inner conflicts lurking inside us. In this chapter, I will help you learn how to unearth the inner conflicts and fears that are limiting your ability to make choices and actually change. One of the first steps is allowing yourself to feel and experience all of your emotions without judgment. Of course, it's about being present in the moment, but also surrendering to the reality of your world.

As I've mentioned earlier, anxiety distorts reality. It changes the way we view situations and interactions with people. It will make us see monsters where there are none and even if they are small and manageable, we will make them bigger and scarier than they need to be. Similar to a distrustful mindset we will see dangers in the world where none exist. I will teach you how to manage your emotions so you aren't reacting, but instead finding your inner calm and tranquility. It's not as simple as willing negative emotions away, but about being mindful when faced with difficult choices. One of my favorite quotes is by the Greek philosopher Heraclitus who wrote, "The content of your character is your choice, day by day, what you choose, what you think and what you do is who you become." Fearlessly and mindfully taking the step to face our fears is a step toward freedom of choice and capturing our potential and finding our purpose in life.

Surrendering Is *Not* Quitting

As I walked out of the hall, still processing my humiliating experience, I noticed the event's guest of honor, Mohamed Makkawy, a former Mr. Universe and runner-up to Mr. Olympia. He was surrounded by a mob of fans trying to purchase an autographed picture. I couldn't help but think this could have been me one day. Feeling both envious and rejected, I wanted to approach him and start a conversation—but that wasn't going to happen. I was too embarrassed and I would've had to wait in line for something I couldn't afford both emotionally and financially. So I stayed in my corner in admiration. As the crowd started to dissipate, I was able to get closer to Mr. Makkawy. It is then that he and I stared at each other. *What should I do?* I'm thinking. *Do something!* my inner voice ordered. Surrendering to the chatters inside I timidly waved at him in hopes of a response. Then something incredible happened. Mr. Makkawy signaled that he wanted me to approach, and I gladly complied. Feeling my heartbeat going faster with each step I took, I found myself face to face with one of the greatest champions of all time. "I watched you perform onstage," he told me, "You have great potential. Don't give up because you didn't qualify. It's only by losing that you can be a winner."

What great encouragement he offered. Those kind words have given me much comfort through the years. At that moment, I went home and avoided discussing my losing experience with my family. I avoided my father, as I felt he might belittle and deplete what little reserves of confidence and soul power I'd managed to store up. I also avoided going to the gym. I buried myself in my accounting studies, as it was almost time for graduation. I knew, deep in my soul, that I was letting my fear of failure affect my spirit and athletic pursuits. In my academic life, however, I succeeded and earned a degree in accounting. I wanted to pursue my studies, but my parents had other plans for me—namely marriage.

Although my father married my mother out of love, it was customary in both my parents' families to arrange their children's marriages. Imagine my shock when one summer's day 1981, barely nineteen, and right after my graduation, my father told me that I was to marry Sahra, a beautiful seventeen-year-old girl from Algeria whom I'd met just once. She was the daughter of my mother's distant relatives; we were to be married the following week.

I protested and told my father that he had no right to force me into marriage.

You are my son and I want the best for you," he replied calmly. "You are to be married in a week."

The humiliating competition experience was easy next to what was to come.

According to the rules of his North African Nomad's culture, marriage makes a man achieve full manhood. My mother also felt that this match would ensure me with a happy and responsible adulthood. One problem was that I had grown up in modern French culture where people lived more independently and married according to individual wishes. In my culture, they married later and for love.

Besides, I was too busy searching my soul for the real Nordine—trying to fix my self-image and life goals—to submit to an arranged marriage. As a first-born son, however, my loyalty to my parents was severely tested, and I felt under great pressure to fulfill their wishes. During the few days before my mother returned with my bride-to-be, my father and I argued about the marriage. He spent much time convincing me that getting married to Sahra was the right decision. His stubbornness wore me down, however, and I reluctantly agreed to go along with my parents' plan and prepare for my wedding day.

In my heart of hearts, I despaired over marrying someone I neither loved nor knew. But my loyalty to my parents compelled me to cooperate. What a dilemma: while this marriage would satisfy my parents, who I loved very much, it would also put an end to my personal fulfillment. I felt my hopes and dreams scatter into thin air, as if caught in a desert sandstorm.

The day before my mother returned with Sahra from Algeria, my father told me that I was to pick them up from the airport. Well, I slept in that morning, and awoke to loud knocks on my bedroom door. I was late and my father was furious. I hurriedly dressed in the suit my father had bought me a few days earlier and rushed to the airport. As it happened, the plane was late; I treasured those few extra minutes of freedom.

As I waited nervously at the gate with my father, I hoped that only my mother would be getting off the plane. No such luck: as soon as my mother and Sahra materialized and we all said hello, my mother asked us to wait while she and Sahra used the restroom. Imagine my shock and disbelief when Sahra walked out dressed in a wedding gown. Apparently, we were to be married later that same day!

When we got to the car, my sisters had already decorated it for our nuptials. As I was both groom and driver, and very scared about the unfolding melodrama of my wedding day, so it was a rough ride in more ways than one. Poor Sahra. I could tell she felt just as frightened as I did. When we arrived back home, the house was full of guests and the musicians were ready to play. My father had organized everything behind my back so there was no way I could escape. I asked him to give me a few last hours of liberty before going through with the marriage.

Feeling trapped and terrified, I spent the time before the ceremony drinking heavily with my friend Nasser at a local bar. My hopes and dreams swirled out of reach as I recounted my miserable ordeal. The only thing Nasser could do was call my father to take me back home.

Enraged at my condition, my father eventually got me back to the house for the ceremony. Afterward, he ordered me to join Sahra, who was waiting for me in my parents' bedroom. As I was quite drunk and frightened, just getting into the room took enormous effort. (My family followed ancient Berber wedding customs. Thus, Sahra and I were expected to stain the bedsheet with the bride's blood and provide "evidence" of her virginity to the wedding guests.)

When I finally entered the room, Sahra sat on the edge of the bed, continuously repeating, "I am a virgin and I have a medical certification." I understood that she was hoping to protect herself from what people might say if I did not perform. My cousins and father fed me tea and peanuts for a few hours in the hopes of sobering me up. Eventually, the marriage was consummated and I managed to throw the bloody bedsheet over the upstairs balcony. All the women shrieked with joy; the men cheered in celebration and my parents basked in the glory of it all.

From that day forward, I lived two separate lives. I studied and worked out during the day and then went home to my wife and immediate family in the evening. My wife never had the option of an education: in Northern African Berber culture, a woman is trained to work in the house and prepare for caring for her future husband and children. Having grown up in France, where women worked outside the home, I had not expected to live this way; Sahra and I were living according to our parents' beliefs, not ours.

In retrospect, assuming these traditional roles against our respective wills inhibited Sahra and me from expressing our needs as individuals and as a couple. Although we co-produced three beautiful boys and one girl, who we dearly love, my wife and I grew apart both emotionally and socially.

While the love I have for Sahra is very precious and I still consider her to be one of my closest friends, our bond eventually broke due to the unbearable pressures involved with surmounting our cultural differences.

Although we tried everything to save our marriage, including five separations, I believe that she would have had a better life if her marriage had been arranged with someone from her own country who shared her beliefs.

While our marriage ended for the best, my bodybuilding career picked up speed in 1983. I find tremendous comfort in the following quote by Masaru Emoto: "If you feel lost, disappointed, hesitant, or weak, return to yourself, to who you are, here and now and when you get there, you will discover yourself, like a lotus flower in full bloom, even in a muddy pond, beautiful and strong."

The overwhelming stress, doubts, worries, fear, and anxiety I had to endure positioned me to find the best tools to combat the effect of stress on my body and mind. It's only by coming to the awareness that there are always two answers to a problem—a human one and a spiritual one—that I was able, each time, to do my best, surrender, and find calm. Most people confuse surrendering with quitting—it's not! Surrendering is doing whatever you can to the best of your ability and letting it go, then taking a step back to let it do its thing. Quitting means that you no longer have the mental, emotional, and physical capacity to go on—you quit! In the following pages you'll find powerful tools you can use to make stress work for you—not against you.

Stress Is Good If You Know How to Use It

"Man suffers only because he takes seriously what the Gods made for fun."
—Alan Watts

Knowing how to deal with stressful events is at the core of effective stress management. When faced with difficult or challenging situations, we either react and fight back or embrace them and respond with creative energy. This energy can only come from a place of awareness. Paying attention to your thought process is key to redirecting and reframing your mindset.

As I continue to say, life is not about what happens to you but how you deal with what happens. You can deliver the same message or respond to a certain challenging situation with a different and non-threatening attitude. That's because your thoughts trigger your feelings and emotions; they then dictate your actions. Your actions create your attitude. When we face hard choices or difficult situations, we tend to either react or respond positively by being proactive. The good news is that we have the choice to be either; I choose to be proactive most of the time. It's all about the delivery!

Ever since my client Richard lost his job, which was a week before our call, he was still furious and confused. During our session, I instructed him to think positively about his challenging and life-changing situation—difficult to do under the circumstances. To calm him down, I asked him to be proactive and reframe his situation by thinking he'd lost his position, not his job. This new mindset allowed him to be at peace with his challenge. Within a week he had gotten a new position at a competing company where he applied his skills, knowledge, and experience he'd learned at the previous position. Richard gained something from his situation; he lost nothing as his old conditioning suggested. It would of have taken Richard more time, energy, and unnecessary stress to find a new position had he stayed in a negative and reactive mode.

Reactive (standing in opposition):

- You are letting outside circumstances disturb your inner peace.
- You are attached to the outcome and your behavior is driven by fear.
- You are distracted and ineffective.

Proactive (surrendering):

- You are remaining engaged with the situation at hand but detaching yourself from the outcome.
- Your behavior is calm and peaceful.
- You are focused and effective.

Stress Is Part of You

Stress is an integral and important part of our lives, and it has a specific purpose. When you know how to use it to your advantage, managing and reducing stress becomes an important tool to attain higher performance and optimal health and well-being. One guaranteed way to increase stress is to . . . well . . . stress about it. Just reading about its devastating health effects is enough to make you take note. We set unrealistic goals to be stress-free. Rather than eliminating stress, which is impossible and foolish, let's focus on minimizing its harmful effects. "We are not only well equipped to deal with daily stressors, but we can use our behavior to reduce the stress that is harmful," said Dr. Hans Selye, the twentieth century's leading authority on the subject of stress and its impact on human health.

Not All Stress Is Bad: Distress vs. Eustress

Our susceptibility to stress varies, and it is not the same from person to person. An event that causes toxic stress in one person may not trigger it in another. Experiences must interact with a wide variety of background factors to create and manifest as an illness. Among the factors that influence the susceptibility to stress are genetic predisposition, coping style, type of personality, and social and environmental support. When we are facing a problem, we assess the seriousness of the issue and decide whether we have the necessary resources to cope with the situation. If we establish that the problem is serious enough and we do not have the resources necessary to cope with the situation, we will perceive ourselves as being under stress and will, therefore, trigger a physiological response such as sweating, increased heart rate, and increased blood pressure. It is our way of reacting to situations that make a difference in our susceptibility to illness and our overall well-being. Research shows that resilience is the result of individuals being able to interact with their environments and the processes that either promote well-being or protect them against the overwhelming influence of risk factors. I had plenty of resilience which helped me along the way.

Not all stress is bad, however. When the body uses stress to overcome fatigue or to enhance performance, the stress is positive, challenging, and therefore healthy. Stress is good when it forces us to adapt while warning us if we are not coping well and if an immediate lifestyle change is necessary to maintain optimal health. This action-enhancing stress gave me, as an athlete, the competitive edge. This kind of stress is called eustress.

Stress is bad when the demand exceeds our ability to perform or cope, creating fatigue and behavioral or physical issues. This harmful and toxic stress is called distress. Distress causes us to overreact and leads to confusion, poor concentration, and anxiety, resulting in lower and worse performance.

The key is to recognize the good stress (eustress) from the bad stress (distress) and adapt to the one that serves you most. Aligning your life and living on purpose allows you to discover ways to adapt and identify what needs your attention and your energy most. Then address that instead of stressing about things that are not important to you. Most people think of stress as an emotional state that occurs when you go through a negative situation, which is not true. Eustress or positive stress is short in duration, can be exciting, and often motivates and energizes you. It brings opportunities for growth.

Distress lasts longer, creates fear, anxiety, and doubt, and offers an unpleasant feeling. It is a performance and productivity killer to go along with health consequences. Issues like financial problems, divorce, poor grades, and negative arguments can be debilitating. The ability to cope with and manage stress can make a big difference in the quality of your life, and will most likely help you live longer and happier. Because not everyone has the same reaction to particular events or situations, categorizing stressors into two lists of those that cause eustress and those that cause distress can be difficult. But we can still create a list of stressors identified by the general population as negative or positive.

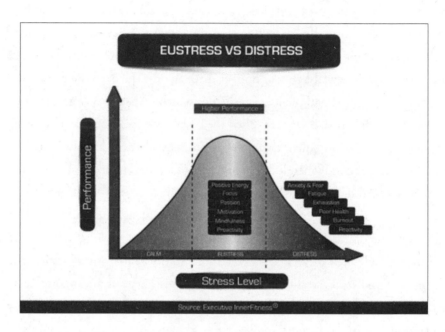

Examples of eustress: Getting engaged or married, a newborn baby, lottery gains, moving or buying a home, going on vacation, retiring, getting promoted or receiving a bonus or pay raise, participating in sport competitions (if you are ready), starting a new job, studying for a test (as long as you keep your eyes on the prize and are not overwhelmed).

Examples of distress: Death of a loved one, divorce, job loss, illness, sleep issues, micromanagement, bankruptcy of financial problems, conflicts in relationships, children's poor performance at school, deadlines, overwhelming job demands, overscheduling, unscheduled or unproductive work meetings, negative colleagues or energy vampires, lack of job training or instructions, nonproductive activities, separation from loved ones, legal concerns, fears or phobias, negative thinking pattern, unrealistic expectations.

Fear or Concern: Escaping from Your Mental Prison

Confusing one for the other can cost you your health.

When you're terrified, you panic, overreact, and tell people how frightened you are rather than taking prudent measures. I've even seen people searching the Internet seeking answers that, most of the time, triggered more fear and anxiety. This is a dangerous and vicious cycle. Let me tell you about a client of mine, Robert.

Robert decided it was time to open up and share his most haunting experience. He took the courage to dump his fears, which sounded more like concerns. Robert shared with me he'd been going through so much emotional and physical pain the last few years that he felt hopeless and could no longer function in the real world.

> "You are what you believe!" —Oprah Winfrey

Robert's issues started when, on a morning brisk walk, he felt out of breath. He was thirty-two at the time and had no preexisiting health concerns. What should have been an easy-to-address issue turned into a full-blown panic attack. Not knowing what was happening to him, Robert searched his symptoms via online forums instead of consulting with a doctor. He spent hours and days seeking answers about what he now believed was a life-threatening condition or illness. The results of his frenzied search led to a psychological roller coaster and triggered a slew of other psychosomatic symptoms he didn't have before.

From shortness of breath, Robert was now experiencing chest and stomach pains, palpitations, nausea, insomnia, skin rash, you name it. He'd create symptoms instantly, just by the mere fact of reading them on various online medical and anxiety forums—yes, the mind is that powerful. He was so terrified to see a doctor or seek help for fear of finding out he had a serious illness. Chronic anxiety took hold of Robert's entire world. His mind was full of dreadful thoughts. He did not realize he was creating a mental prison without walls in which he'd been locked up for years.

Robert's life became a living hell. Both his professional and personal life were affected by his obsessive behavior. He grew desperate to find a real solution. Bringing him back to a place of calm—which allowed for greater awareness— he was able to recognize that his symptoms were in fact non-threatening physical sensations resulting from emotional distress. What Robert needed was to seek professional medical advice, so I asked him to meet with his doctor and make sure there wasn't any underlying illness creating those symptoms. In doing so, Robert would feel an instant relief.

> "What we don't know exists cannot be dealt with."

I am not qualified to diagnose clients with mental issues, nor would I try playing the role of a therapist. But I do, however, have both the experience and qualification to coach and advise clients about their wellness and fitness needs. I can check their current behavior and help them reach greater health and wellness. Because of my professional advice and Robert's newly found strength and courage, he could now seek help. His doctor ordered several medical tests, which were all negative. The simple fact of discovering he was healthy, and that he had no underlying conditions, saw his anxiety symptoms disappear; he realized he just needed a break.

My prescription of yoga, meditation, physical exercises, and a well-rounded healthy nutritional plan, as well as a meaningful connection with family and friends became part of Robert's new lifestyle, and are contributing to keeping his emotional and physical distress at bay.

> **Warning**: If you suffer from anxiety, stop researching your condition—unless you know what you're searching for—visiting online forums to diagnose yourself, or trying to understand your symptoms, as it can make your problem worse (as anxiety can mimic other serious health conditions).

The 90-Second Emotional Loop

Jill Bolte Taylor, a brain scientist and bestselling author of *My Stroke of Insight*, explains in her book that when one reacts to something in their environment, there's a 90-second chemical process that takes place in the body; after that, any remaining emotional response is just the person *choosing* to stay in that emotional loop.

Something happens in the external world that triggers chemicals to flush through the body, which puts it on full alert. For those chemicals to flush out of the body it takes less than 90 seconds. So, during that time, you can watch and feel the process happening; you can feel it, and then you can watch it go away.

After that, if you continue to feel fear, anxiety, anger, etc., you can actively choose different thoughts from the ones that are re-creating the circuitry resulting in you experiencing this physiological response over and over again.

How to Effectively Use the 90-Second Loop

Surrender to the immediate feeling by allowing yourself to experience it. Acknowledge it without owning it; it's going to happen either way. However, now you know you have 90 seconds to divert your attention to a more positive and relaxing focus while your immediate physical response runs its course. You have 90 seconds to switch your thinking.

A powerful way that works for me is to take deep, slow breaths as I allow myself to connect to the present moment. But you can find your own diversion technique—do whatever you can to get through the emotion: count, step up and down, do push-ups for 90 seconds. You can also use a mantra such as, "I have more than enough time to focus and relax."

Now just imagine Robert who, for four years, spent his life in hell because of a simple concern, which turned into fear and into chronic anxiety exacerbated by a lack of appropriate action. Robert could have simply seen a doctor when he experienced his first symptom. Like Dr. Bolte said, it was his choice to stay in that emotional loop far beyond his 90 seconds. The door to his mental prison was open all along. All he needed was to walk out.

Opening Up Your Mental Prison

If you feel anxious and don't know why, take the time to *divert* your thoughts and focus on a positive; something or someone that makes you feel hopeful. Being optimistic or passionate about something good in your life can help ease anxiety. Sharing your perceived fears and opening up to someone you trust can help unravel your false fears.

When people show their deepest thoughts and feelings about stressful or traumatic experiences, negative emotions such as depression and anxiety lessen and eventually disappear. Those who open up are less likely to become depressed and are less susceptible to the harmful effects of stress. That's because they can face their fears at their own pace, in small doses, and with someone they trust.

Numerous studies show that people who report a greater reliance on spiritual beliefs and who are also involved in healthy social interaction during times of stress have an emotional, mental, and physical health advantage over those who do not.

Gratitude and Anxiety

Sometimes we just need to stop thinking about what's next and appreciate what's here now.

Gratitude can decrease feelings of fear and anxiety. Psychologists Dr. Robert A. Emmons of the University of California, Davis, and Dr. Michael E. McCullough of the University of Miami, have done extensive research on gratitude. In one study, they asked all participants to write a few sentences each week, focusing on specific topics.

One group wrote about things they were grateful for that had happened during the week. The second group wrote about daily frustrations or things that had upset them. After 10 weeks, those who wrote about gratitude were more enthusiastic and felt better about their lives. They also exercised more and had fewer visits to physicians than those who focused on sources of aggravation.

Appreciate what you have, while you are pursuing what you desire.

Managing Stress: Take Control

When society's demands exceed your ability to perform, it's difficult to stay committed to your heart's desire, goals, and even your core values. Balance is important if you want to regain control of your well-being. If you feel your life is overwhelming, the solution should *not* be to seek external brain numbing tools such as binge-watching TV, tobacco, alcohol, drug, food, or unhealthy sex.

Seek better and meaningful behaviors that combat stress, not add to it. It is well documented that both mental and physical exercises are the most powerful tools for combating stress. Do whatever it takes to get to the gym, but don't kill yourself exercising. While physical activity helps with decreasing tension and elevate your mood, it can also add to it if you are overdoing it, as the stress of exercising can be just as harmful as stress from other sources. This often happens when we're overtraining. How much exercise is the right amount depends on the individual, but there are warnings of overtraining, and these are sure signs you're doing too much. In fact, these are *real* signs of overtraining or over-stressing: fatigue, elevated blood pressure, a weakened immune system, sleep problems, anxiety, depression, loss of appetite, trouble concentrating, and so on. They are certainly indistinguishable from the symptoms associated with chronic stress from other sources. Not knowing what to do or how to use gym equipment can also be a source of unnecessary stress.

Instead, be mindful, ask (or hire) someone to show you the best modality, and, most of all, allow time for recovery. Mental and physical exercises, as well as sleep and dietary choices, are important and most powerful when combined to reduce stress and anxiety. Movement and activity offer a diversion, getting you away from the source of stress and anxiety to clear your mind and allow you to sort through the problem. Regular exercise also makes you look and feel better about yourself.

Physiological changes that occur with long-term regular activity supplies you with additional strength, endurance, and energy to cope with difficult situations. Muscular tension, which builds up throughout a stressful day, is released with aerobic activity and stretching. Research has shown that exercise can reverse or improve many of our stress-related health problems. Benefits include lower blood pressure, lower cholesterol, improved sleeping patterns, and lower body fat. According to Dr. James Alan Blumenthal, PhD, a clinical psychologist at Duke University (from his 2007 article in *Psychosomatic Medicine*) exercise is generally comparable to antidepressants for patients with major depressive disorders.

Try New Things

What works for you may not work for someone else—one person may enjoy yoga, while another may feel calmer after running. Pay attention and determine what works best for you. Here are 50 of the most powerful and effective stress-reducing tips that help me and many of my clients:

1. Know who you are.
2. Connect with your self-worth.
3. Love yourself.
4. Practice self-compassion.
5. Make a list of your core values.
6. Avoid stressful people and situations.
7. Focus on the positive.
8. Be proactive.
9. Surrender to and embrace change.
10. Brake the panic or anxiety cycle (breathe and divert your thoughts).
11. Find a passion.
12. Be grateful.
13. Do what you love.
14. Try new things.
15. Volunteer.
16. Adopt a pet (if you are an animal lover).
17. Stick with integrity.
18. Have more fun.
19. Have a good laugh.
20. Have a good cry.
21. Smile often.

22. Know your expectations and adjust them when necessary.

23. Ask for help when you need it.

24. Connect with others.

25. Spend quality time with family.

26. Practice mindfulness.

27. Meditate.

28. Practice deep breathing.

29. Do yoga.

30. Exercise with weights.

31. Do cardio.

32. Eat small, balanced and healthy meals.

33. Drink plenty of water.

34. Sleep better and longer. (If you suspect you might have sleep apnea, please see a doctor.)

35. Learn how to say no and delegate.

36. Be flexible.

37. Pick your battles.

38. Be willing to compromise.

39. Nurture yourself.

40. Spend time in nature; sit under a tree.

41. Manage your energy, not your time.

42. Trust in yourself.

43. Listen to music.

44. Watch less TV.

45. Learn more.

46. Read more.

47. Make good love.

48. Express feelings instead of repressing them.

49. Address mental issues if you suspect them.

50. Take more vacations or time off for yourself.

Optional: Schedule an annual health checkup (especially if you know you need one).

Useful Tips: Taking time out when things get tense may be a great idea. I find deep and slow breathing exercises to be a very effective stress-reducing tool. Here is how to do it: Breathe in slowly and deeply through the nose, and breathe out through the nose. Do this for three minutes.*

In the next chapter, "Body," you'll learn how your body can be your greatest asset to regaining inner peace.

---

* See Golden Rule #2: "The Three-Minute Box Breathing Technique," in chapter ten, for additional information.

Part II

Synergy: Your Mind, Body, and Spirit Connection

CHAPTER SEVEN

BODY

Be proud of your body.

I WAS THE last speaker at a conference. The list of speakers and thought leaders who spoke before me were very impressive, and each speech was inspiring and thought provoking. All the attendants were diligently taking notes and asking questions. It was an intellectually stimulating environment. When it was time for me to get up on stage, I looked at the audience and said, "Everything you have learned this weekend is useless. Useless." I paused, and finished my thought, "If you don't take care of your body."

We want to diminish the role of the body, but the fact of the matter is without it we are unable to navigate the world. Addiction, lack of sleep, lack of exercise, and intense stress all affect our ability to live life to the fullest. Life is a contact sport. Whether we are contemplating a huge merger at work, buying a new home, or starting a job, our body will take a blow. It's best to make sure it's working well.

In most self-help books, the body is neglected. We talk at length about the spirit and the mind while completely ignoring our physical fitness. In this chapter, I will weave into the conversation the importance of taking care of your body and starting a relationship with it. Our body is a temple. It's our first defense against the world, so we need to be aware of what we eat, how much we sleep, and how much we drink. We have to be ready for anything the world can (and will) throw at us. Using examples from my time working with Alzheimer's patients for the Alzheimer's Research and Prevention Foundation, I will offer advice on how to begin a spiritual connection to your body. Also, how to be inspired to exercise, eat right, and sleep enough, and not just force yourself to be motivated. Getting motivated for some of us can be close to impossible, but if we are inspired to make a change, it will come not only naturally, but easily.

Remembering My Friend Bill

Bill can't remember his name, but he knows what he wants. He wants to arm wrestle with Mr. Universe and take him to the floor and give him a lesson. That's what Bill wants.

I was part of the three-day brain longevity program, working in collaboration with Dr. Dharma S. Khalsa, founder and medical director at the Alzheimer's Prevention Foundation. Bill was one of the eight patients seeking treatment and attending the seminar, and was introduced to me by both Dr. Dharma and Bill's wife, Carole. Bill and I immediately connected at a deeper level; it was like we had known each other for years. I felt incredible warmth coming from him; his deep blue eyes projected a sense of peace, even a sense of happiness.

There were four facilitators, a medical doctor (Dr. Dharma, MD), a registered nutritionist (Luz Elena Shearer, RN), a yoga teacher (Kirti K. Khalsa, Dr. Dharma's wife), and me (fitness and wellness specialist). We were working as a team to help cognitive-decline patients, like Bill, to either slow down the progression of the illness or prevent it. The onset of Alzheimer's can start as early as 20 years before any symptoms can manifest, which is before you even know you are afflicted with the disease.

"Bill, this is Nordine, he is Mr. Universe and he will take care of your muscles," Carole said.

"Mr. Universe? Really?" Bill said while reaching to touch my biceps.

"I have big muscles, too! Look!" He said with a huge smile.

The team and I were swapping patients, with each of us simultaneously seeing a different one. The office I used was a room at the hotel where the seminar took place. There was enough space for Bill to grab me and throw me to the floor like it was nothing. Bill was strong and still had tremendous coordination despite being diagnosed with Stage 5 of the disease: moderately severe decline.

While on the floor we played like two kids. Carole was in tears.

Before the devastating illness, Bill, a strikingly handsome man, was a polo champion. Professionally, he was the founder and CEO of a multi-million-dollar company. He had it all: four-hundred-acre horse farm, a beautiful wife, and two amazing children. But Bill was, like many high achievers, plagued with anxiety and needed something to calm him down after work—so he drank. It is well documented by a slew of researchers that high stress along with alcohol, drug addiction, lack of proper nutrition, lack of quality sleep, and lack of exercise can all contribute in the development and progression of Alzheimer's. This is why we taught a program that combined yoga, mind/body connection, meditation, nutrition, and medical treatment. It was an all-around powerful synergy.

One morning, Bill woke up not remembering a thing. Everything was gone. He was just fifty-four years of age, and his entire life crumbled right in from of him—though he was completely unaware. The disease took over and, in a blink of an eye, Bill had completely lost control.

I got to know Bill better after traveling on several occasions to his farm in Michigan to work with him. The Bill I knew was a bit different from the Bill others perceived. I looked at a man who despite losing most of his brain capacity was gentle, loving, and a pleasure to be with. His energy invited me to drop the professional mask and just be me.

There was no fear, no ego—just Bill.

From that state of being, Bill was able to live the rest of his life like an innocent child who lost his mental health but regained his authenticity. We don't have to suffer from a debilitating condition to be authentic, we just need to detach from the outcome of any situation that stresses us out. We need to be engaged with our self-worth and detach from our external world while doing our best to be at the service of humanity. Detaching from the world does not mean becoming a recluse—to the contrary. You are contributing in making that world a better one simply by protecting your own sanity. You are being yourself, loving yourself, and loving others. The Bill I got to know and work with helped me look at life though a different lens. I see clear now, I see the real me contributing to the betterment of humanity while creating an inner and better landscape that allows me to rejuvenate and recharge when I need it. I am a better person with better capability to help. I am able to remove myself from negative situations by making better choices. Sometimes we enter a situation by default, but we always have the choice to detach from it.

My regret is that I would have loved to know and work with Bill before the illness took over. Or maybe I should be grateful that I got to help him in spite of it.

It sucks getting old, it really does. As we get older, our body takes a toll; we can feel the wear and tear as we journey through life. While scientists have found mental decline happens in our forties, most bodily functions go downhill after our thirties—our metabolism slows down, our bones and joints weaken and, if we're lucky, we can get up to six hours of good sleep. That's if we've taken care of ourselves and made smart and healthy choices along the way.

If not . . . well, there is no need for me to get into the details of the negative effects of growing old and unhealthy. It is possible, however, to navigate this journey while minimizing those effects. I say negative because I believe getting old is not bad at all! You're wiser, you have more time to spend with your loved ones, and you're not chasing your tail anymore—if you gained awareness of who you are, that is!

When your life is in a state of equilibrium, it doesn't matter what your status is, how old or how healthy you are. What matters is that you know how to make the necessary adjustments when life strikes and you get off balance. Young or old, we all dread misfortune—it's an uninvited guest we'd rather avoid.

If It Doesn't Itch, Why Scratch?

I love my dog, King; an adorable Frenchie full of energy. King and I have a special relationship. I talk and he listens (for the most part), we walk, we run, and we play together. King's favorite thing to do is steal my socks and underwear so I can chase him around the house. I assure you it can be both amusing and frustrating.

One gorgeous and sunny morning, after successfully getting dressed—that's without chasing him around—King and I went running together on a path

Myself at age twelve, moments before my (very late in life, and almost life-threatening) circumcision. (center: my uncle, Merrat; right: my brother, Ahmad)

Posing for a picture at age twenty, two weeks after gymnastic event. Notice that my left wrist is broken due to an injury sustained while competing on the pommel horse.

With my gymnastics team and those supporting us on.

At twenty, posing for the Paradise Gym hall of fame, a day after a humiliating defeat at my first competition in Belgium.

Working out moments before a photo shoot in Singapore, and five months before the world championships in Berne, Switzerland.

Winning the WABBA 1986 World Championships. (center: myself; left: Justin Jospitre; right: Christian Benathan)

At twenty-five, upper-body comparison between myself and Arnold Schwarzenegger. Note that these are just picture comparisons to illustrate the importance of visualization. Arnold was instrumental, as he was the object of my inspiration/goals for many years.

Posing for *Linea Sports* magazine after hiking almost two hours in the beautiful scenery of Rimini, Italy, one day after my first 1991 IFBB Professional Grand Prix. I came in 2nd.

The goals of positive visualization. Upper left: me pretending I am having my own book signing at a Barnes & Noble in Tucson, Arizona. Upper right: me signing my own book, *Mind Over Body*, two years later at the exact same Barnes & Noble. Lower left: me at age twenty, in my bedroom. (Notice the pictures of famous bodybuilders on my wall. Same people I beat in competitions just a few years later.) Lower right: me at age twenty-four, after the Mr. Universe competition in 1986. Yes, the powers of visualization and affirmation work wonder when you drop all doubts and fears, which is a part of *InnerFitness*.

Me and boxer hall of famer Sugar Ray Leonard after a training session, 2003.

Me and actor Charlie Sheen during a training session, 2000.

Me before a meditation and Kundalini yoga session. It's part of my own daily *InnerFitness* practice.

Meditation—one of the pillars of mindful fitness, and a core element of *InnerFitness*.

Basic spinal energy series: Sat Kriya (Kundalini yoga).

Basic spinal energy series: pulling Mulbandh (Kundalini yoga).

Basic spinal energy series: Easy pose, shrugging (Kundalini yoga).

Basic spinal energy series: Bear grip sea saw motion (Kundalini yoga).

Quadriceps stretch.

Shoulder stretch.

Hamstrings stretch.

Salutation pose (yoga).

Cat stretch (hip, back).

Cobra pose (spine and core stretch).

In 2019, speaking at an International convention in Phoenix, Arizona, energizing a room full of young engineers ready to get to their next level of *InnerFitness*.

November 17, 2006: celebrating with my daughter, Isabella, the day I became a US citizen. Very moving experience; I went from dreaming about America when I was little and while watching my favorite John Wayne movies to actually being sworn in as an American. Dreams do come true, and believing is key to achieving them.

My friend, my companion:
King and I relaxing after a walk.

surrounded by the beautiful Catalina Mountains, in Oro Valley. Upon returning home, King refused to go up the stairs to our home. "Come up, buddy! Come up!" I shouted. Like most dogs, King loves to stay outside; I don't blame him, especially on a beautiful day such as this one. Suddenly, as he complies and runs up, his leash catches my foot and causes me to trip. I felt my right knee popping; it wasn't very painful, just slight discomfort. I didn't think much about it until the next morning, as upon stepping out of bed I felt a sharp pain radiating across my knee (though I was able to manage and go on with my day). A few days passed and the pain increased, as did my concerns. I was afraid I'd injured myself. To be sure, I scheduled an appointment for the next day with my orthopedic surgeon.

Upon examining my knee, the surgeon made his diagnosis. "I think it might be a meniscus tear, Nordine.".

"What? No way!" I answered frantically. Fearing for the worst, I asked, "Do I need surgery?"

"It's probable, yes. I'll order an MRI to make sure."

You can imagine the chatter in my head as I waited for the MRI results. It can be hard for anyone to cope with injury, which mainly has to do with the recovery period. A full recovery can take up to a few months depending on the severity of the injury and the rehabilitation. When you own your own business, these misfortunes can cause serious setbacks. I wasn't spared! This would bring me down—*again*! But this time I had the awareness and knowledge I didn't have before the injury I'd suffered 17 years earlier. To cope with my ordeal, I used the same tools I am sharing with you in this book.

On May 1, 2019, I had arthroscopic knee surgery. It took less than 30 minutes; no major damage, just a small tear. "You did great, Nordine!" the surgeon said. "Just take it easy and you'll be able to walk without crutches within two days." He then prescribed ibuprofen and oxycodone as needed. I was reluctant to take any pain meds, as I knew of the devastating effects of a full-blown addiction to them. I tried to avoid taking them—I thought I wouldn't need them—but I was also warned that as the effects of the anesthesia would subside, I would feel pain . . . *and pain I felt!*

This was an outpatient surgery, so I was out of the clinic in less than two hours. As advised, I used crutches so I could move around. "Icing, icing, icing!" was my doctor's recommendation, not to mention the pain meds, one every four hours, as needed. "Stay ahead of the pain and take your pain meds" was my doctor's warning. The day went by and I did not need any pills until about 10 p.m.

As I was getting ready for bed, I began to feel an excruciating pain. I couldn't fall asleep, so I gave up and took a pill. Shocked and desperate that it didn't work, I had to take another one—this time not only did it kill the pain but also knocked me out. I was afraid that the pain would return, so I complied with the doctor's recommendation and took the meds every four hours. When I say the meds, I mean the hardcore meds, the oxy! Ibuprofen wasn't doing anything for the pain.

My experience with opioids could have been disastrous. Although the meds helped with the pain, it also affected me psychologically; it numbed my feelings. I could not focus on my work. I was feeling short-lived euphoria—which made me feel detached from reality.

Disaster Avoided

You don't need an addiction expert to tell you that anyone who takes opioids is at risk of developing an addiction. There are several factors—such as genetic, psychological, and environmental—involved in addiction. Although using opioids such as oxycodone for just five days causes a sharp increase in the likelihood of developing dependence, for many people it can lead to a lifetime of addiction. It was an exceptionally turbulent period of my life that put me at higher risk of using the drug long term. Living in the states, it wasn't easy for me to deal with my family whom most resided in France. With my mother's serious illness and my younger brother's coma—not to mention my history with anxiety—it was enough to put me at the edge of addiction.

As the days went by, I began feeling an irresistible craving for the meds. Even though I was no longer feeling strong physical pain, I continued taking them; every four hours as the doc prescribed and as needed—*and I needed them*! I needed the drug to release endorphins in my brain and boost my feelings of pleasure. I wanted to feel that powerful sense of well-being. The same sense of well-being I would feel after 30 minutes of exercise. Since I wasn't able to get an effective workout due to my injury, I had no choice . . . or so I thought.

The Day I Faced Reality

As I recounted in a local ESPN interview, it was the eighth day since the surgery that I realized I was setting myself up for disaster. I woke up around 6:30 that morning, and for the previous few days I'd been waking up agitated; my body still wanting to rest but my mind not wanting to let it. I felt physically and emotionally exhausted. It is said that what troubles you during the day hunts you during the night, and that's exactly how I felt.

I was troubled—who wouldn't be? Finding yourself dealing with nursing an injury, checking your mom and brother's serious conditions from five thousand miles away, managing your business, and tackling other daily tasks. My mind was racing like a roadrunner and, like the coyote, I couldn't catch it. My daily morning meditation routine normally did the trick, but now it wasn't.

Finding just enough mental and physical strength to drag myself out of bed and into the bathroom, I opened the medicine cabinet and reached for the oxycodone bottle, ready to pop a pill. Like most people, I have a healthy habit of checking myself in the mirror, though that morning I made the effort not to do so; I avoided my usual self-encouraging stare and went strength for the bottle. As I removed the red cap, I noticed a warning I hadn't read before: "Caution; Opioids. Risk of overdose and addiction." It's at that moment that I remembered how addiction had destroyed both my brothers' lives, leaving them both with organ failure. Both had serious addictions to heroin and alcohol, and also recalled my client Roger's battle with addiction (which I'll share in this chapter) and whom I helped break a nasty six-year habit with Vicodin and alcohol. With these intense memories resurfacing, there was no way I would allow myself to jeopardize my health, my family, and my career. I looked up and stared at the mirror. Since I knew that the eyes reflected our unconscious mind, and that they are the windows to the soul, I looked into my own eyes and asked: *What are you doing? Why are you even thinking of taking this poison, you don't even have pain anymore? You don't need this!* This powerful self-enquiry would trigger self-compassion and allow for inner truth.

Without waiting for an answer—afraid of rationalizing my way back to taking the meds—I began a countdown to 10, 9, 8, 7, 6, 5, 4, 3, 2, 1 . . . and here I am, back to reality. I threw the bottle back in the medicine cabinet and I grabbed the crutches, limping my way out. *I've traveled the four continents four different times. I beat illness, overcame bullies and anxiety. This will not take me down!* I'm affirming. Two thousand steps later, which is an enormous achievement after only a little over a week since my surgery, heart pumping and my blood flowing, I felt good. I declared the end of my dependence to the pain meds. I said "no" to addiction.

> "Tragedy has the power to bring us down, yes, but we possess within us an even greater power to overcome anything—just find your way back to InnerFitness."

I'm thankful for the knowledge I had, which helped me calm down and take my recovery one step at a time.

So why did someone like me, who teaches others to be healthy, be more aware, and more mindful, have to go through this kind of experience? I had the tools to avoid it to begin with. Well, I'm human and I, also, make mistakes. All I can do for you in this book, as I do with my clients, is provide the tools and teach you how to use them so you can gain the courage and awareness to acknowledge your mistakes, correct them, learn from them, and move on with your life.

It's precisely because I have the knowledge and awareness to get me out of this unfortunate and dangerous situation that I did just that, and avoided a potential disaster.

Into the Abyss of Addiction

Happily married and the father of two children, Roger is a strong and handsome young man; at twenty-nine years of age, he stands 6-foot-4 and weighs 250 pounds. A former linebacker for his college team, he is well accustomed to injury. Roger's favorite stress reliever is to ride his motorcycle—he treasures his

Kawasaki Ninja. To blow off steam after a long and stressful day, he prepares to indulge and gets on his bike. Sadly, this would be his last motorcycle ride for years to come.

Roger zips out of the garage and off he goes. In just a few minutes he is racing on the Tom Landry Freeway in Dallas, Texas. It's 6 p.m. and the freeway is filled with rush-hour traffic. About 10 miles later, attempting to exit the jammed freeway, Roger puts on his signal and makes a slight left turn—that's all he remembers as he wakes up at the hospital. A concussion and a chattered right leg is the doctor's diagnosis. Roger got into a terrible accident; he had been blindsided by a pickup truck.

The youngest of two boys, Roger came from a very successful Texas oil family and was the president of the company his father founded. As one can imagine, working hard wasn't a necessity to him. Roger was the next in line to be the CEO of another company the family owned. You can only imagine the amount of stress he felt, sometimes working more than 70 hours a week and with little time left for his personal life.

"I feel like I can't slow down, Nordine," he said during our first one-on-one phone consultation. "My stress level is through the roof. I feel tension taking ahold of my entire being the instant I get up in the morning. And since my motorcycle accident I have problems with sleep, I'm super anxious, and I've gained over sixty pounds. I need serious help." he shared with extreme frustration.

"It's like being on my bike going 150 miles an hour, every day, all day long, and I can't stop it. I don't want to crash like I did six years ago." Roger was metaphorically making a reference to the motorcycle accident I shared earlier. An accident that would bring him and his loved ones so much pain and hardship.

He was recalling a very turbulent period of his life and felt very emotional, so we had to take a brief pause. As we resumed our session, Roger was having a very hard time speaking about the ramifications of the accident and how it ravaged his life. This terrible and unfortunate event seemed to still be in his shadow. Depression, weight gain, marital troubles, and work issues were discussed in our one-hour session, but there was no mention of addiction . . . yet.

Roger was already working with a trainer but wasn't fully committed, and the reason he'd contacted me was because his father, who was also a client of mine, thought it'd be a good idea that he'd consult with me. After listening deeply to him I deemed to ask Roger—as I do with most clients who require my full and personal attention—if he would consider coming to Miraval to relax, recharge, and work with me for a week. He fervently agreed. "I need this badly," he said.

Upon checking into the resort a couple of months later, I greeted Roger and showed him the premises. The next day we started with the usual morning meditation, behavioral assessment (self-worth, beliefs, feelings, core values, etc.), fitness evaluation, and workout session. Everything was going great.

It was 5 p.m. when we met at the resort's restaurant to have our first dinner together—as I usually do with my clients at least once during their stay. I immediately noticed that Roger was exceptionally euphoric; I was expecting him to be more relaxed. As we sat down at the table, he immediately ordered a glass of wine. After just a few seconds, it occurred to me that Roger was already half drunk. I was astonished, as the resort's alcohol policy was strict; guests were only allowed to drink between 4 and 10 p.m., and only within a specific area called "The Brave Bill." He must've begun drinking in his room during our two-hour recess. How did he manage to sneak alcohol onto the premises? I also silently pondered on the idea of leaving the table but, out of respect—which he obviously lacked—I stayed.

"Would you like a glass of wine, Nordine?"

"No, thank you. I don't really drink."

"Ah, OK!" "Maybe I shouldn't either?"

"It's your choice, Roger."

"Anyway, how are you on this lovely evening, Nordine?"

"Very good, Roger. And yourself?"

"I am super excited to be here," he replied as he took a sip.

As the conversation evolved, so did his drinking. Roger was becoming very talkative, excited, and even confused. I had to do something, say something, as I was growing wary and felt uncomfortable with our conversation, which was quickly turning into a loud and disruptive one-way discussion. To Roger's astonishment, I cut the dinner short and escorted him to his room.

"OK, Roger. Time to go back to your room so you can rest. We'll reconvene in the morning. Besides, we both need to get a good night's sleep, we have a long day ahead tomorrow," I instructed him.

"But why?" he asked. "I am having fun here, did I do something wrong? I'm not drunk!"

"It's nothing, Roger. Let's go."

"OK, OK! Can I get one more glass of wine?"

"No, Roger. That's enough, you don't need it, let's go."

I realized that evening that Roger had no sense of self-worth—he was hurting! He seemed to be operating from a very low level of existence: doubt, anxiety, fear, and anger were ruling his life. He was completely detached from reality and seriously needed an emotional connection, observations I could make based on his behavior. My commitment to help Roger became clear that evening. We met the next morning at 8 a.m. at the Kiva, a sacred meeting place built by Native Americans, surrounded by the majestic Catalina Mountains. That beautiful and sunny morning after our morning meditation, Roger made a confession that would save his life.

I'm not sure if it was guilt or shame of the night before, or that he felt he could trust me enough to let it all out and share his destructive and deeply held dark secrets. While it's true, that people are inclined to share their weakness or struggles with those they trust, the serene environment should also be taken into account. The mammalian brain (which is responsible for emotional safety) opens up, thus enabling the person to be emotionally safe. While Roger was talking, I noticed that he was holding something in the palm of his hand.

"How do you feel, Roger?"

"I feel better now that we meditated. I'm sorry for last night, I behaved like a jerk! I woke up this morning to a very sad message from my wife, Loren. She's leaving me!"

I could see the pain on his face, and did my best to console him.

"I am so sorry to hear that, Roger! I really am!"

"I need to change my self-destructive ways, Nordine."

"That you do, Roger. But only *you* can make that happen. Can I ask what you're holding in your hand?"

"Sure. This is a picture of my daughter, Nicki, and my son, Tommy. They're four and six," he answered with a choking voice. "I can't lose my family!"

"Can I ask you something, Roger? And please be honest."

"Of course!"

"Last night's drinking . . . is it a habit?"

After a long pause, he answered: "Yes. I wish it was the only thing."

"The only thing?"

"I think I am slowly killing myself."

Preparing for a confession he had most likely not spoken to anyone else, he continued.

"I am going to share something with you and please keep it to yourself. I'm addicted to painkillers. I take sixty Vicodin a day and I drink a twelve-pack of beer regularly. It's bad, Nordine!" he confessed.

"After the accident, I was in so much pain for so long, I was desperate. I got addicted. It was the worst time of my life. I am spending a lot of money on these drugs—and now I'm deep into it."

"That's bad, Roger, I'm sorry! How long has it been?"

"Since the accident, six years. I gradually raised the dosage to sixty tablets, though."

"Have you asked for help? Does anyone else know? Your family, friends?"

"No, except for the alcohol. Everyone thinks I stopped the meds years ago. My wife may suspect I'm still taking them, though, but not sixty!"

"How about Nicki and Tommy?"

"What about them?"

"They get in your car, right? You drive them around?"

"Yes, I do! To school, soccer, and tennis practice!"

"Can I see that picture again?"

"Sure, here it is," he answered, handing me the photograph.

"They are so beautiful and so innocent. Do you want to lose them?"

"God no, of course not!"

"They, and many others, could be collateral damage of a war you are losing." You are putting them in direct danger! Wake up! Lives are at stake, Roger! Not only your kids' lives, but yours and others' as well."

Desperately, Roger said: "I know, Nordine. I know, and that's why I want to put an end to this."

"I am glad to hear that. It will take some work, some things I will help you with, and others you must seek professional help. But in order to even begin the process, you must first connect to your self-worth. You need to fight and win! You must focus and make a choice to win this battle. Do you want to win or lose?"

Roger looked intensely motivated and answered: "I want to win!"

"Good! You know that ultimately your life will be defined by the decisions you take and the series of choices you'll make along the way. Up until now, lord knows you've made some bad ones because you lacked the knowledge—you didn't know better, you didn't know you'd fall so low. It's time to rise above and fight back."

The rest of the week went by quick—too quick for both of us, if you ask me, as Roger and I began to bond on a deeper level. We were both fathers with children of similar ages, and that made it much more powerful. I had tremendous compassion and empathy for him. Roger was on his way to a long and full recovery from what was killing him—his addictions. It took two rehab stints and one relapse, but eventually Roger would win his battles with alcohol and opiates. There was collateral damage, however: his marriage. Roger split with Loren but maintained a civil relationship. Except for his sixty-pound weight gain, unnecessary stress, and minor health issue, no one else was (physically) hurt, and eventually Roger would marry again and start his own company.

A huge part of his recovery process was my coaching—it helped with reestablishing harmony in his life. Roger would get to spend more quality time with his loved ones, lose the unwanted and dangerous extra weight, and regain the sleep he desperately needed. Although those were major wins over significant battles—to win the big war—Roger had to make a series of hard but good choices and repeat them over and over. Choices such as changing behaviors, including taking care of his body.

Dr. Gabor Maté, an expert on addiction, says all addictions originate in trauma and emotional loss. Roger was experiencing trauma caused by his motorcycle accident and had lost his sense of self-worth. As a result, he neglected his body; it is no surprise that he was feeling depleted.

In the following chapter, I outline a comprehensive approach to dealing with your most valuable asset: your body. I base this concept on my many years of experience in working with clients who needed to create a work-life balance. I realized that many of my clients were spending their days in their minds and outside of their bodies—living in fear, worrying, stressing, analyzing, thinking, and judging. This approach emphasizes on the synergy between all four aspects of one's life—not just the physical. When the body works in harmony with the mental, emotional, and spiritual aspects of your life, you experience well-being.

CHAPTER EIGHT

THE FOUR PILLARS OF MINDFUL FITNESS

There are four essential parts to a whole being.

I BELIEVE THAT to live a meaningful life, we must learn to balance its four basic aspects—physical, emotional, mental, and spiritual—by honoring the importance of each one and setting goals for achieving each aspect's optimum health and fitness. If you're familiar with traditional Chinese philosophy, you have heard about the ancient concept of balancing yin and yang—the two opposing forces found in all things in the universe—to optimize chi, or life force. Ayurveda, the traditional healing philosophy from India, is also based on finding a balance in your mental and emotional states, and connecting with your spirit to heal your body.

I base my philosophy of living life in balance on ancient wisdom I don't believe that you have to reject material things to achieve well-being, but I do believe that you need to find a balance among all four aspects to feel good about yourself and find true happiness. Think of those aspects or states as reservoirs that need to refill with energy before they're emptied. If you don't put gas in your car, you'll run out. The same holds true for your life: if you don't recharge your energy spent, you'll get burned out.

Remember Roger in the previous chapter? When he came to see me at the resort, he'd depleted most of his reservoirs and had reached dangerous levels, thus creating both conscious and unconscious self-destructive habits that would bring him down to a very low level of existence.

Although Roger would get on a path to full recovery from drugs and alcohol, it was only by combining therapy and the tools outlined in this book that his success was possible. His rehabilitation wasn't easy, as he had developed bad eating habits and wasn't exercising. This is often the case with individuals trying to battle an addiction—they swap one habit for another. Roger would gain weight because of poor eating habits, lack of sleep, lack of exercise, and unmanaged stress.

I don't think anyone needs to hit rock bottom before they can awaken to reality; accepting one's current life situation is key to moving toward healing. I'm glad Roger reached out and was honest enough to open up. Together we worked to address all four aspects of his life. Using these methods, Roger regained moment-to-moment equilibrium.

Regardless of what you are dealing with, implementing the information outlined here and throughout this book will help you restore optimal health and well-being back into your life.

Physical Fitness:

- How healthy are you?
- Are you eating balanced and healthy meals?
- Are you getting enough restful sleep?
- Are you exercising three to five days a week?

If the answer to any of these questions is no, then you are not receiving your optimum energy and, most likely, will get tired during your workday, therefore hindering your focus and productivity. Not taking care of yourself will deplete your *physical fitness reservoir*.

Signs of Physical Stress:

- Clenching your fists
- Squinting your eyes while staring at something (computer screen,
- smartphone, document)
- Excessive teeth grinding
- Jaw clenching
- Muscle tension

Maintained for long periods of time, these physical manifestations could potentially be damaging to your nerves.

Boost Your Physical Fitness by:

- Exercising regularly
- Eating healthy small meals
- Getting 7 to 9 hours of sleep each night
- Napping
- Hydrating throughout the day
- Avoiding unhealthy addictions such as alcohol, fast food, drugs, tobacco, or sex.
- Taking your daily vitamins/supplements

Emotional Fitness:

- How happy are you?
- Are you feeling upbeat?
- Are you enthusiastic?
- Are you optimistic?
- Are you happy?
- Are you feeling energized?
- Are you in touch with the loving and creative part of yourself?
- Are you free from anxiety, doubt, fear, or depression?

Taking stock of your emotional well-being is a must if you want to perform at a high level and create optimum productivity.

Boost Your Emotional Fitness by:

- Meditating
- Being mindful and maintaining awareness of thoughts and feelings
- Nature walking
- Building a circle of meaningful and trustworthy friends
- Avoiding energy vampires
- Say "no" more often, and when necessary
- Developing a passion
- Opening up to new things
- Having a healthy romantic relationship
- Having a healthy sex life
- Spending time with family
- Listening to upbeat or relaxing music
- Taking vacations
- Adopting a pet

Mental Fitness:

- How well can you focus?
- Are you feeling drained or are you feeling mentally sharp most of the time?

Your mind contributes largely to your energy levels. Having high levels of mental energy will provide you with better focus, greater awareness, improved willpower and motivation, and increased productivity. Your mind has a surprising effect on your physical energy, as your thinking pattern also affects the way others perceive you and how you perform. When you feel self-confident, you look self-confident. Your performance will increase—multiplying, therefore, your chances of success in whatever you are doing. One sure way to feel instant and long-lasting self-confidence is not to rely on others' validation, but to know you already have all you need; you have self-worth, you have life, and with that you can do, be, or have anything you set your mind to.

Boost Your Mental Fitness By:

- Thinking positive
- Being mindful
- Surrounding yourself with people, not better but smarter than you
- Surrendering to what is
- Clearing your mind
- Meditating
- Reading stimulating books
- Doing puzzles (many smartphone apps are available for mind games)
- Reading positive and relevant articles in the paper
- Traveling (traveling is the antidote to ignorance)
- Having fun more often (see my note on COVID-19 at the end of this book)

Spiritual Fitness:

- What is your purpose?
- Do you yearn the need to connect with nature?
- Are you driven by something other than the material world?
- Do you feel connected to others?
- Do you love unconditionally?
- Do you care about the world?

Your spiritual energy is your life force—or chi—and is the acceptance of the divine love within yourself. It is the bridge that connects mind, body, and soul. Spiritual energy is everlasting and available through prayer, meditation, or simple contemplation.

Boost Your Spiritual Energy by:

- Having a sense of self-worth
- Being grateful
- Praying
- Meditating
- Doing yoga
- Finding a passion
- Practicing acts of kindness
- Hiking a mountain
- Learning a new skill or a new language
- Reading
- Listening to relaxing music
- Going on a journey
- Volunteering to help a cause

As you can see, all four pillars are crucial to our well-being and are paramount to our functioning at an optimum level. When we lack harmony between them, we put ourselves at risk of not living a full and happy life.

Next, I'd like you to focus on your commitment to change and find out how ready you are both mentally and emotionally by learning more about your will-power and taking the "Five Stages of Behavioral Change" test below. By assessing your readiness, you're likely to stick to a plan for long-lasting health and well-being. In my ten-year tenure as Miraval's Fitness and Wellness director, this is the one test people neglect to take, therefore diminishing their chances for success.

Your Willpower Muscle

If you find yourself struggling with your commitment to exercising or to maintaining healthy diet don't be too hard on yourself. According to neuroscientists, a lack of willpower is *not* a character flaw, and it could all be down to the physical structure of the brain. The part of the brain, called the prefrontal cortex, is the same part that records our working memory and is in charge of willpower.

Researchers have shown that when the brain is overwhelmed with tasks, its willpower can weaken.

The solution is not hammering people with new habits, but helping them bulk up their willpower muscle by making them consciously aware of certain changes that need to take place before any physical habits are set in motion. In other words, you must outsmart the subconscious mind and make firm conscious decisions to commit to your goals while being sure to keep your word with yourself. If you put exercising last on your daily list of your to-do list, you will fail. You will be so tired—both physically and emotionally—that outsmarting your subconscious will be almost impossible. So make sure you make an appointment with yourself to exercise before work or in the middle of the day. The same holds true for your professional life. You must schedule your most important tasks first. For those who can't find the time to exercise before or in the middle of a workday, have a set of exercise clothing ready and go straight to the gym or your outdoor activity location.

> **Warning**: Don't stop at home after work—unless you exercise there—or go to dinner, as it will compromise your willpower.

The Five Stages of Behavioral Change: What Stage Are You In?

"Preparation is key to success."

As a coach and speaker, I frequently give advice about changing habits. Even though many of my clients can change in the *short term*, most of them revert back to their old conditioning. So what are some effective ways to permanently change behavior?

According to research on smoking conducted by Dr. James Prochaska, a professor of psychology at the University of Rhode Island, there are five different steps (or stages) to changing habits in your life. These are: pre-contemplation,

contemplation, preparation for action, action, and maintenance. These stages will help you determine if you are serious about getting things done, getting organized, getting healthy, or are just fooling yourself, as you may have done many times in the past. See if any of the following statements sound familiar.

Pre-Contemplation

You have no intention of changing your behavior. You are unaware of your problems.

At this stage, there are probably members of your family or friends that are trying to make you change, yet you insist that all is well. As far as you're concerned, you don't have any problems that need changing.

Contemplation

You know that a problem exists and are thinking about overcoming it, but have not yet put a plan to do so into action.

Like many, you could spend a long time—sometimes years—in this stage. But a coach or a mentor might inspire you. You are looking for ways to change, but just need a push in the right direction.

Preparation for Action

You have unsuccessfully taken action in the past year, though intend to take further action in the coming weeks.

At this stage, you're committed to taking the right course of action. Most people who need to change their behavior never get to this stage or progress beyond it.

Action

This stage involves obvious behavioral changes and demands real commitment and energy. You are definitely motivated at this stage.

At this stage, it's crucial that you pay attention to the slightest changes; how you feel or look will inspire you to stay the course. Small baby steps are the ones that count most. You are doing fine, but wish you could do more.

Maintenance

You are working to prevent relapsing to old negative habits and are combining the gains achieved during the action stage. At this point, you're seeing real results and are determined to make them long lasting.

Be mindful that at this stage you are still vulnerable; you can still relapse. Even though you've created new habits, the old ones are still there in your head. Stay away from old conditioning. You're looking for external motivation to maintain your changes. As long as you keep up with your new habits and behaviors, you'll be fine.

I'd like to think that you're reading this book because you're in the contemplation, preparation, or action stage. Regardless of which phase you are at or want to get to, be mindful that you are investing in your health or paying for it later. It's a conscious choice you must make if you want to improve your life. Meaningful and long-lasting changes are only possible when one is ready to act and build strong and healthy habits. Everything we do is a matter of habits, and learning how to make new ones can be tricky for some. Creating good habits will allow you to stay on the path to a life in balance.

Mindful Habits: How to Build Them and Make Them Stick

"The beginning of a habit is like an invisible thread. Every time you repeat the act, you strengthen the strand. You add to it another filament with each repetition, until it becomes a great cable and binds you irrevocably to each thought and each act. First, you make your habits, and then they make you. Your thoughts lead you to your purpose. Your purpose always manifests into action. Your actions form your habits. Your habits determine your character and your character fixes your destiny. Your habits are either the best of servants or the worst of masters."

—Orison Swett Marden, inspirational author
and founder of *SUCCESS* magazine

Ninety-three percent of what we do in a single day is ingrained in our subconscious mind; what we do is a process of repeated conscious behaviors. In order to successfully implement a healthy routine in your life, you must give up old habits and replace them with new and healthier ones. When you start a diet, you don't just eat healthy foods without eliminating the unhealthy ones.

I think anyone truly committed to change their lives need to learn new habits—it's a huge and necessary part in the process of behavioral change. I know a thing or two about building new habits, after all, getting to the top of my game required me to create a solid structure in my life, without it, it would have been impossible for me to climb the ladder of international stardom.

Anatomy of a Habit

In his *New York Times* bestselling book *The Power of Habit*, author Charles Duhigg explains that individuals and habits are all different, and so the specifics of diagnosing and changing the patterns in our lives differ from person to person and behavior to behavior. In the first chapter, Duhigg shares that MIT researchers discovered a simple neurological loop at the core of every habit, a loop that consists of three parts: a cue, a routine, and a reward.

Understanding your habits requires identifying how your loops work. Once you have established the habit loop of a particular behavior, you can look for ways to replace old vices with new, healthier routines.

Obviously, it would be unfair for me to simplify the content of Duhigg's wonderful book, so I'm going to share my personal experience of what I've learned about my own habits and those of my clients, and how we successfully changed them.

Essentially, begin by asking yourself if your habits are serving you well, if they are aligned to your core values, and if they are moving you closer to your goals. The sum of your habits controls the outcome of your life, playing a huge factor in your happiness. They make you fit or fat, healthy or unhealthy, happy or sad. Your success depends on them. So it's fair to say that improving or replacing your old vices with new behaviors should do the trick.

There is a framework very similar to Duhigg's that I use when realizing that a habit is not working for me:

- I identify the trigger responsible for my behavior (cue)
- I recognize the behavior that led me to take action (routine)
- I acknowledge the reward of my action (reward)

Once I understand the framework, I ask myself what other trigger and behavior would help me get the same or similar reward. Changing the trigger (or cue) and the behavior (or routine) is crucial to forming a new and better habit.

Let's use my Roger as an example:

Roger had developed night binge eating. Ben & Jerry's chocolate ice cream was his new drug (sometimes devouring two pints) while watching his favorite TV show every evening after a hard and stressful day at work. (He knows that he is not matching his action with his core value of being fit and healthy, but it's a strong habit.)

What's his trigger (or cue)?

Television

What's his behavior (or routine)?

Eating Ben & Jerry's ice cream

What's his reward?

Feeling good (until guilt sets in)

I helped Roger in replacing his bad habit and reform a new one: stop eating at 7 p.m. and immediately brush his teeth with strongly flavored toothpaste.

New trigger (or cue)

Set a reminder to brush his teeth by 7 p.m.

New behavior (or routine)

*Brush his teeth with a strongly flavored toothpaste while reading his core values**

Same reward

Feeling good both for not eating ice cream and for being consistent with his core values.

---

* Most people won't feel like eating after brushing and especially after confronting themselves with who they aren't, hence reading their core values is important.

Roger could have chosen many other healthier reminders, such as eating a healthy snack, reading, going for a walk, calling a friend, taking a shower, or waiting for 15 minutes until the craving went away.

If your intention is to be fit and healthy but your habit is to eat junk, guess what? You are not being true to yourself; your behavior is not matching your intent. So if you feel anxious about things you know you shouldn't be doing, ask yourself if your action is matching your thoughts. Cultivate the right mindset by deciding to change from the inside out. When you have self-worth and the right self-image, you'll do what's conducive to your health and well-being. The process will become faster, healthier, and easier than you ever imagined it could be.

Since successful people are those who build healthy habits and routines, I suggest you think of building one for yourself. The following will help you do just that.

Build a Morning Ritual: Start Your Day Feeling Energized, Recharged, and Fully Engaged

"Since the nature of people is bad, to become corrected they must be taught by teachers and to be orderly they must acquire ritual and moral principles."

—Xun Kuang, Chinese Confucian philosopher

Routine vs. Ritual

There is a big difference between a routine and a ritual. To most, a routine is getting up every morning and doing the same mundane tasks day in and day out; eat breakfast, brush your teeth, take a shower, and go to work. It's not very glamorous, but these things are important and need to get done. And for most, these activities can be boring and require effort.

However, rituals are more meaningful and purposeful practices. Often, there is a rooted yearning to be more, and a real sense of fulfillment attached to rituals. They are soul-feeling practices, as opposed to worldly feeling activities.

Here are the key differences I find between routines and rituals.

Routine:

- Worldly feeling
- Require effort
- Fear driven
- Dutiful
- Outside motivation
- Disengaged
- Focus on task or activity

Ritual:

- Soul feeling
- Effortless
- Love driven
- Celebratory
- Inner motivation
- Fully engaged
- Focus on the performance

Having a ritual is the secret to self-development, high performance, and productivity. There is a certain power to a ritual. It's easy to get lost in a daily routine when your day is overwhelmed by tasks and personal obligations. We spend precious energy and time figuring out what needs to be done, and by the time we do get our first task we already feel drained.

Rituals help you get in the zone, help you build a healthy framework, and lead you to become more than if you didn't have them. They remove all the guesswork and put you on the right track. Having a ritual makes you feel energized, recharged, passionate, and engaged in what you're doing. You and the task at hand become one. Unfortunately, many people rarely get into a zone; they are everywhere and nowhere simultaneously. Most successful people I've met and worked with all had some ritual or rituals.

Take my father, for instance; he had several rituals. To raise *thirteen* kids, he had to work hard. Busting his butt day in and day out for 30 years at the same company. To get to work he'd walk two hours to and from his job, working eight-hour shifts. My father was illiterate and never went to school but, boy, was he courageous. Despite the mountain of challenges, he and my mother did an excellent job sending me and my siblings to college. Without his rituals, my father would have lost it. He had a morning ritual to get him going, a storytelling ritual where he would gather with friends and relatives and inspire them so they, too, could protect themselves against the burden of challenges, a Sunday sauna ritual, and a prayer ritual to get him connected to his religious beliefs. I'm grateful to have learned from him; he helped me see life from a different perspective.

I also have several rituals: a morning ritual, a workout ritual, and a bedtime ritual. Because I take a day off from work, my Sunday rituals differ slightly from my weekdays' rituals.

Here is how I start my weekday (when I'm not traveling for seminars or workshops):

6:30 a.m.: Wake up, make bed

6:45 a.m.: Shower, brush teeth

7:00 a.m.: **Morning Ritual** (meditate, breathing exercises, visualize the day ahead, read, review goals)

8:00 a.m.: Prepare and eat breakfast (protein shake or eggs with fruits and vegetables)

9: 00 a.m.: Writing posts, articles, or manuscripts

10:30 a.m.: Snack: Greek yogurt and nuts; client call

11:00 a.m.: Research new trends on health and wellness

12:30 p.m.: Lunch (cook or eat out, generally healthy foods)

2:00 p.m.: Back to my office; client program design

3:30 p.m.: **Afternoon Ritual** (warm-up, strength training, cardio, stretching, post-workout shake)

4: 30 p.m.: Writing, preparing material for seminars or speaking engagements

6: 00 p.m.: Leave office; personal time (family or socialize with friends)

7: 30 p.m.: Dinner (with family or friends)

9: 00 p.m.: Unwind (kids, watching TV, reading)

10:00 p.m.: Evening Ritual (listen to classical music in bed, candle and incense lighting)

10:30 p.m.: Lights out

Carving out some alone time and preparing your week ahead of time allows you to see and feel everything you need to focus on for the upcoming week while eliminating the unnecessary stress, distractions, and guesswork. You'll feel clearer and more energized to start your week. You'll have more energy and time to enjoy what matters to you and your loved ones. You'll live a life "on purpose and on target." Next, let's get on with the "golden rules of mindfulness."

The Golden Rules

Now that you've learned more about replenishing your reservoirs and are ready to take action, it's time to go over some of the most important activities I consider essential for attaining long-lasting health and well-being. I call them the "golden rules," and they are: *sleep, breathe, eat,* and *move.* Practice and implement them in your daily life and experience an optimum state of InnerFitness—that's my promise to you!

CHAPTER NINE

GOLDEN RULE #1: SLEEP

Sleep For Emotional, Mental, and Physical Recharge

"Sleep creates harmony between our health and our bodies."

THIS IS A big one! Sleep-related problems affect up to 70 million Americans. Most of my clients complain about a lack of sleep or sleep problems. Remember Roger? He was getting a whopping four hours a night! At one point or another in their lives, most people will experience some kind of sleep issue. When I was under tremendous stress and anxiety, I experienced insomnia, so I know first-hand how devastating it can be to suffer from a lack of sleep. Although stress and anxiety can cause sleep disturbance, sometimes finding balance is key to re-establishing a healthy sleep routine.

How Much Sleep Do You Need?

It's not the amount of sleep we get that's important, but rather the quality. Even though most sleep experts and medical doctors alike are recommending seven to nine hours' sleep a night for adults, It's still not clear how much one needs as there are many mixed studies on the right amount. Some say six hours is enough. I even heard Arnold Schwarzenegger say, "You don't need more than six hours of sleep to be at your top." Even successful people such as Richard Branson, Martha Stewart, President Barack Obama, Marissa Mayer, President Donald Trump, Tim Cook, Howard Schultz, and Kelly Ripa to name just a few, all sleep less than six hours a night. You think some of these people need to be at their best so they can do their jobs as world leaders and influencers? Are they at their top as Arnold claims? I have strong doubts—and for good reasons. Although I am not judging or criticizing some of these amazing people, I think they may be out of the norm; they are *extraordinary*!

So, What's the Big Deal About Being Sleep Deprived?

Gloria is a successful international lawyer in her mid-forties and a partner at a law firm in California. At the time we worked together, she had a work schedule that left her only five hours to sleep. Her life was spent in airports and offices, and she found herself in a constant state of tiredness that had become her norm. Gloria felt comfortable in being miserable. She thought she was one of those extraordinary people who could get by sleeping little and doing a lot . . . and that was true for about 15 years, until one eye-opening day came crashing down on her.

It was 8 a.m. when Gloria collapsed at the Miami International Airport. Luckily she was OK; she hit nothing on her way to the ground. She had collapsed from exhaustion, and while she didn't have a heart attack or stroke, it could have been worse. That day changed Gloria's life forever. She decided to re-evaluate everything as it was time for balance. While reassessing and reorganizing her life, Gloria discovered that lack of sleep not only was damaging her health, but ruined her marriage and left her without any meaningful friendships to speak of. All she had was work.

Like many, Gloria thought she was a successful individual (to a degree). But as you know by now, success isn't measured by how much money you have or even by your titles or recognitions. **Success is health.** It's the way you feel from morning to night. There are only a few people, maybe 3 percent of the population that can function on only a few hours' sleep.

For the rest of us, it's easy to run on caffeine or other stimulants to shut down our natural alarm that says, "I need sleep, please!" But eventually, you will pay the price for fooling yourself. I've seen it way too many times to count; you feel pressured by the need to be performing at a high level and meet the demands of both your professional and personal lives. You want to achieve your goals, cram as much work into your schedule as possible, and be successful while burning the candle at both ends—because that's what you'll do to attain the pinnacle of success. There is nothing wrong with that except you can't do it on five hours a sleep a night! And even if you do, it won't be long lasting. Why? Because you can't catch up on sleep; it'll catch up with you—and that's a fact.

In today's society, the need to be more and achieve more by performing at a consistently high level has become not only the norm, but also an obsession. We are constantly pushing ourselves, timing ourselves, and stressing ourselves to do and be better. Because of the growth in technology, our lives have become "information saturated." We're bombarded with distractions such as text messages, pop-up notifications, emails, social media comments, and online videos. We hate it, yet we crave the euphoria of being busy and in demand; it's an addiction. Unfortunately, we are also distracted.

These distractions are overloading our minds. We walk around with our brain in a fog while we search for our favorite coffee or energy drink and hope for a moment of clarity. We make ourselves push through these constant interferences in our day-to-day living that are hindering our quality of life because we don't know how to disconnect. In desperation, we add yet another app to our phone hoping this will make things better . . . yet it only becomes one more thing for us to do. What's bothering you during the day now torments you at night, therefore robbing you of much-needed sleep.

As I've said, I've seen it happen to many of my clients. The ramifications of poor sleep will ultimately bring down what you've work so hard for.

What I am asking you to do here is to change your beliefs about sleep by reassessing your priorities. Think of sleep as the fuel that keeps you healthy and full of energy so you can achieve ultimate performance and continue achieving your goals, aspirations, and dreams. When you are full of energy, you accomplish more without jeopardizing your health.

You Need Your Deep Sleep

Deep sleep is not only important, it's vital to one's health and ability to function optimally. You need anywhere from one-and-a-half to two hours of deep sleep per night, which is about 20 percent of your overall sleep. Listen to your body and you'll know how much sleep you need. Monitor yourself by tracking your sleep time and quality until you know works best for you. Some studies show that the duration of total sleep is not what causes us to be refreshed upon rising in the morning, but rather the number of complete sleep cycles we go through. Furthermore, a host of new research studies suggest that this stage of sleep can help reduce levels of beta-amyloid and tau, two hallmarks of Alzheimers disease. Each sleep cycle has five distinct phases with different brain wave patterns. The following is an attempt to give you an idea of what those stages are.

Sleep Cycle Explained

Non-REM Stage One (Drowsiness)

NREM1

This is the first and lightest phase of your sleep cycle. In this phase you are between wakefulness and sleep. Your heart rate begins to slow and, as you're dozing off to sleep, you are aware of sounds but are unwilling to respond. No dreams here.

Duration: 1 to 7 minutes

Non-REM Stage Two (Light Sleep)

NREM2

In this phase you're asleep for the first time. Your brain activity, heart rate, and breathing begin to slow down, and your body temperature falls slightly. You are not able to recognize sound content. This phase consists of most of your sleep time.

Duration: 10 to 25 minutes

Non-REM Stage Three (Deep Sleep)

NREM3 & 4

This is your deepest sleep of the night. During this phase your brain activity, heart rate, and breathing are at its lowest. This is a very important stage for body repair, regeneration, and strengthening of your immune system. It's difficult to wake you up in this stage, but if awakened you'll feel groggy and it will take a few minutes to recover your mental ability. You're not aware of sound or stimuli.

Duration: 20 to 40 minutes

REM Sleep (Dreaming Sleep)

Before you get into Stage R, you usually get back up to NREM2 for about 5 to 10 minutes. As the night unfolds, each REM cycle increases in duration, with the final one lasting up to an hour. This is that exciting time of the night when you do your most intense dreaming. Your blood pressure, heart rate, and breathing and brain activity increase as your body temperature falls. To prevent from acting out on your dreams, your muscles become temporally paralyzed and unresponsive during this stage. You can become sexually aroused, even if you are not having erotic dreams. This important cycle of sleep is key to mental and overall health and well-being.

After REM sleep, you usually go back to NREM1 or NREM2 and start the whole cycle over again.

Why Do We Need Sleep?

Sleep plays a major role in preparing our body and mind for maximum performance and productivity. At least two significant studies have shown that the less sleep you get, the more likely you are to be overstressed, overweight, and be at a higher risk for diabetes and cardiovascular disease.

In 2004, Dr. Steven Heymsfield of Columbia University and St. Luke's-Roosevelt Hospital in New York, and James Gangwisch, a Columbia epidemiologist, headed a study that looked at the information provided by 18,000 adults.

What the researchers found was that people who got less than four hours of sleep a night were 73 percent more likely to be obese than those who got the recommended seven to nine hours, unless you are one of those rare individuals who needs less. Those who averaged five hours of sleep had a 50 percent greater risk, and those who got six hours had 23 percent more.

In another study, researchers at Stanford and the University of Wisconsin-Madison looked at more than a thousand participants in the Wisconsin Sleep Cohort Study who spent a night in the lab and had a blood sample taken upon awakening. What they discovered was that those who slept shorter times had higher blood levels of ghrelin, a hormone that increases appetite, and lower levels of leptin, a hormone that decreases appetite. The shorter sleepers also had a higher body mass index (BMI), which is used to measure your body mass based on height and weight.

Mental Well-Being and Sleep

Mental illness and sleep are not simply associated, but rather physically linked to the brain, as Professor Russell Foster, head of the Nuffield Laboratory of Ophthalmology and the Sleep and Circadian Neuroscience Institute, explained in his June 2013 TED Talk. Professor Foster said the neural networks that predispose us to normal sleep and those that give us normal mental health are overlapping. Genes that have been shown to be important in the generation of normal sleep, when mutated or changed, predisposes individuals to mental health issues. Professor Foster explained that by understanding these two systems, was have begun to grasp how both sleep and mental illness are generated and regulated within the brain.

So, the long and the short of it would seem to be: take sleep seriously and get a good night's sleep!

Bad Habits That Can Affect Sleep:

- **Alcohol** reduces sleep quality, waking you up at night. To avoid this effect, stay away from alcohol in the hours before bed.

- **Caffeine** can cause sleep problems up to twelve hours after drinking it! Stop consuming caffeinated beverages after 3 p.m.
- **Nicotine** is a stimulant, which disrupts sleep.
- **Drinking** lots of fluids—even water—may result in frequent bathroom trips throughout the night, therefore interrupting your sleep. Although it's important to drink plenty of water during the day, avoid drinking at least two hours before bed.
- **Eating too much food**, especially fatty foods, can compromise a good night's sleep. These take a lot of work for your stomach to digest and can keep you up. Acidic or spicy foods in the evening can cause stomach trouble and heartburn.

Sleep and Your Kids: The Key to Less Stress in Your Life (If You Are a Parent)

The healthier our kids are, the healthier we are. If you are really committed to your kids' health and well-being—as I am for mine—you should consider helping them get the sleep they need. Furthermore, in recent findings, sleep researcher Wendy Troxel explains in her November 2016 TED Talk, that the consequences of sleep loss in teenagers can be disastrous, and waking them up hours before their biological clock says they are ready can deprive them of the sleep they desperately need—literally robbing them of their REM sleep, which is most associated with learning, memory consolidation, and emotional processing. Troxel goes on to say that sleep deprivation among American teenagers is an epidemic; only about 1 percent get the eight to ten hours of sleep per night recommended by sleep scientists and pediatricians.

When they go through puberty, teenagers are experiencing a delay in their biological clock, which determines when we feel most awake and most sleepy. This is driven in part by a shift in the release of melatonin, a hormone that helps control daily sleep-wake cycles. Teenagers' bodies don't start releasing melatonin until around 11 p.m., which is a couple hours later than adults or younger children. "This means that waking a teenager up at 6 am is like waking an adult up at 4 am," Troxel says.

As the late Nelson Mandela said: "Children are our greatest treasure. They are our future." I can't agree more. If we want to ensure that they take the right path to a bright future, we must help our children understand the importance of healthy sleep. To function well, they must get enough sleep—there are simply no other alternatives. I know they want to stay up late to play video games or watch TV, but the price they pay is way too high and can cost them (and you) a great deal of unnecessary stress. For many teens experiencing chronic sleep loss, their coping mechanism is to consume large quantities of caffeine in the form of energy drinks and energy shots. Today's teens are super wired and super tired. Recent research, published in the February 2013 issue of the journal *Pediatrics in Review*, concluded that caffeine-laden energy drinks could cause rapid heartbeat, high blood pressure, obesity, and other medical problems in teens.

Lack of sleep will greatly impair their performance; here are just a few mental, emotional, and physical symptoms (not including the side effects of energy drinks) of sleep deprivation in teenagers:

- Reduced alertness
- Anger and irritability
- Anxiety, depression, and suicide
- Poor problem solving
- Hunger (makes them want to eat more sugary foods)
- Shortened attention span
- Slower than normal reaction time
- Poor judgment
- Reduced awareness of their environment (peer pressure, risk assessment, bad company)
- Poor memory
- Reduced concentration (especially at school)
- Loss of motivation

Keeping our children healthy can have an enormous impact on our own health. Better school performance, better sense of belonging, and a better sense of well-being can produce a healthy family—hence way less stress for parents. I don't know about you, but trying to talk with a teenager who suffers from a lack of sleep is like talking to an invisible wall—you won't get anywhere.

The following indicates that, as we age, the amount of sleep we need changes drastically—so the recommendations vary across a person's lifetime:

Newborns: 12 to 18 hours
Infants: 14 to 15 hours
Toddlers: 12 to 14 hours
Preschoolers: 11 to 13 hours
Elementary students: 10 to 11 hours
Teenagers: 8.5 to 9.25 hours
Adults: 7 to 9 hours
Mature adults: 7 to 8 hours

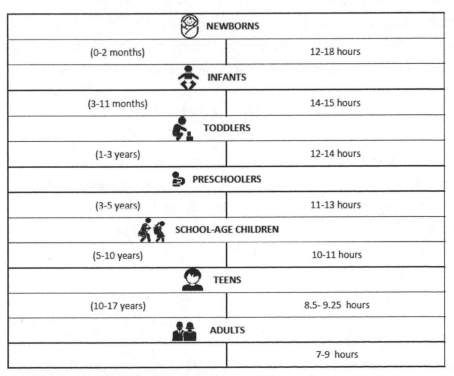

NEWBORNS	
(0-2 months)	12-18 hours
INFANTS	
(3-11 months)	14-15 hours
TODDLERS	
(1-3 years)	12-14 hours
PRESCHOOLERS	
(3-5 years)	11-13 hours
SCHOOL-AGE CHILDREN	
(5-10 years)	10-11 hours
TEENS	
(10-17 years)	8.5- 9.25 hours
ADULTS	
	7-9 hours

(Taken from the National sleep Foundation Web site.)

Note: By getting the sleep they need, your kids will be healthier. They'll also have a greater chance to succeed and enjoy a better quality of living, therefore reducing a great deal of stress in your own life.

Tips for Healthy Sleep

Keep Moving or Take a Warm Bath

Low-impact physical exercise early in the evening, such as a leisurely walk, helps you enjoy more restful sleep. Walking can clear the mind of the day's worries and activities. Many of us can experience "monkey mind," from time to time. I find exercising very helpful in burning that extra energy and assist with falling asleep quicker. A warm bath can also promote sleep for others. Repetitious thinking—such as counting sheep or reciting positive affirmations—works for some people as well. Reading, praying, and meditating can relax the mind, allowing sleep to come. I caution against evening strenuous physical activity, as it can stimulate your nervous system, making it difficult to fall asleep.

Stop Midnight Awakenings

For people who awaken during the night and cannot return to sleep, there are many natural remedies to help with that. Avoid drinking fluids after your evening meal to reduce the need to go to the bathroom during the night or in the early morning hours. People who take diuretics should take them in the morning instead of the evening to prevent nightly bathroom trips.

Don't Touch That Snooze Button!

People suffering from early morning insomnia should attempt to go to bed earlier so that their rest is completed by their morning waking time, rather than remaining in bed and perpetuating the focus on not sleeping. It's best to get up and do a productive activity, as opposed to taking those extra nine minutes for a snooze.

Keep Electronics Out of the Bedroom

Lights out 30 minutes before falling asleep. Let's face it: we love our gizmos and gadgets. I know I do. Our modern society is flooded with high-resolution electronic screens—TVs, PCs, smartphones, and tablets that can be easily taken just about anywhere. Many people find it difficult to disconnect, and more use electronic devices in their bedrooms, which is preventing them from getting the rest they need.

A 2011 Sleep in America® poll done by the National Sleep Foundation found that 6 in 10 Americans use their personal computer within an hour of going to sleep, and 4 in 10 Americans bring their cell phones, smartphones, or tablets into the bedroom. A staggering number of people—80 percent, per the study report problems falling asleep at night, and these devices are likely a contributing factor. This is in part due to the effects of LED backlit screens emitting glowing blue-light wavelength on melatonin, a hormone that regulates sleep and wakefulness.

Build and Follow a Regular Sleeping Ritual

Wake up refreshed and ready. When it comes to following a sleeping pattern, discipline is key. If you are frequently changing your sleeping times, then it will inhibit your body from developing a sleeping cycle or rhythm.

Most people who wake up energized and active are the ones who have developed a regular sleeping pattern; they make sure they get to bed at the same time every day and wake up at the same time.

For example, if you go to bed at 10:30 p.m. and wake up at 6:30 a.m., and make this a habit, your body will get into a sleeping rhythm—also known as the circadian rhythm, which is a 24-hour internal clock that regulates cycles of alertness and sleepiness by responding to light changes in our environment.

Listen to Music and Drift Away

Music can relax you and induce sleep. I love to listen to classical music 30 to 45 minutes before going to bed. My favorites are "Claire de Lune" by Claude Debussy and "Meditation from the opera Thaïs" by Jules Massenet. If you are not a classical music fan, that's fine. Play anything that relaxes you, something like Cafe Del Mar Dreams (Buddha Bar Mix) by Milews . . . just don't listen to AC/DC or something that makes you want to jump out of bed and go dancing or running.

> **Note**: Many people listen to music on their smartphones, and so here's one option I use (specifically on my iPhone, but I'm sure you can do the same with other smart devices). You can play music on your phone, then go to your Clock, click on Timer, and at the bottom the option "When Timer Ends" you can choose "Stop Playing" at the bottom. Now you can play music until you reach the scheduled time and are ready to fall asleep and don't have to worry about it going all night.

Use Guided Meditation for Sleep

I personally find guided meditation to be very helpful and recommend it to all my clients. There are many free guided audio meditations for sleep available on the Internet. YouTube has an extensive reputable selection. You can also purchase guided meditations for sleep and relaxation on CD, at any bookstore, or online. I prefer the app versions so I can have them on my smartphone. I usually use a bluetooth headset and leave the phone in a separate room.

If you suffer from chronic insomnia, consult with your physician as there may be some underlying medical issues causing your sleep disturbance.

Warning: If you suffer from sleep apnea and use a CPAP machine, wear it before listening to guided meditations for sleep.

Myths About Sleep

We Need Eight Hours of Sleep Each Night

Well, not exactly. Some people need more, while others need less. Listen to your body, it will let you know. The number is between seven and nine hours. Some people are still claiming that they can function well on five or six hours; I'd like to know how they manage to stay fully engaged and focused on their tasks!

We Need Less Sleep as We Get Older

Not true! All adults, regardless of their age, need to sleep somewhere between seven and nine hours per night. Their quality of sleep may not be as good, however.

Alcohol Makes You Sleep Better

Although it's true that drinking alcohol before bedtime induces sleep, it also hinders the quality. Alcohol is a depressant that increases non-REM sleep and reduces REM sleep. Not getting enough REM sleep has been linked to poor emotional functioning and extreme crankiness. Trust me, you don't want that if your intention is to be highly focused and productive the following day. And, by the way, it also kills your workouts for the week and lowers your metabolism (if you get wasted that is!).

Sleeping One Hour Less per Night Won't Affect Your Daytime Functioning

You may not be that sleepy during the day, but losing even one hour of sleep can affect your mental ability.

Sleeping More on the Weekends Will Help You Make up for Lost Sleep during the Week

Partly true! It can help relieve part of a sleep debt, but it will not completely make up for the lack of sleep. Furthermore, sleeping later on the weekends can also mess up your sleep-wake cycle.

Five or Six Hours of Sleep Are Enough

Again, and as I mentioned earlier in this chapter, it's absolutely false! Researchers at the University of California, San Francisco, discovered that some people have a gene that enables them to function well on five or six hours of sleep a night. This gene, however, is very rare, typically in less than 3 percent of the population. For the other 97 percent of us, six hours doesn't cut it.

To Nap or Not to Nap? That is the Question!

Napping was paramount to my success as a professional athlete. I took a nap every day regardless of where I was; I would find a place to rest for half hour or so. This allowed me to recover between double-split workout sessions.

It is very common for people in many western societies to sleep in a single consolidated block of about seven to eight hours during at night, but this is not the only sleep pattern.

In many cultures—especially those living in the Mediterranean—afternoon napping is ordinary, and is built into daily routines. We're all familiar with the concept of a siesta, a short nap normally connected to the lunch hour. The siesta is practiced in Italy, Spain, Portugal, and by many other countries.

While visiting Italy many years ago, I was amazed to see that no one worked between lunchtime and 2 p.m.; they all went home to take a nap. My friend Flavio, who was my host in Cuneo northern Italy, called it *riposo*. Even churches, government buildings, and shops were closed during lunch hours. Most people take between 30 minutes to an hour to nap or take a siesta.

Lack of sleep costs US companies a whopping $63.2 billion in lost productivity, according to a September 2011 study from the American Academy of Sleep Medicine. Many companies have expressed a renewed interest in napping, and are even capitalizing on the trend. MetroNaps, a manufacturer that makes napping chairs called "Energy Pods" that are designed for office use, has sold nap pods to companies such as Zappos and Google, to name a few. Today, roughly 5 percent of employers have on-site nap rooms and are encouraging their employees to rest and recharge; this number is expected to rise. Japanese companies are even paying employees to take a snooze at nap cafés.

Obviously, the corporate world is catching up and has realized that napping isn't just for babies; they understand that napping has a huge connection with health, productivity, and performance. Napping recharges your energy.

Napping can help increase you or your staff's performance and productivity, increase morale, and reduce stress. It can help you make smarter and healthier decisions that can reduce health costs, increase vitality, and decrease absenteeism.

Note: According to sleep experts, people with insomnia may make their nighttime sleep problem worse by taking naps, and mostly recommend naps for people who feel they benefit from them.

Think of your bed and how comfortable it is. Avoid any thoughts about sleep while getting to sleep. Your bed is for sleep and sex. Listen to your body and track your sleep to identify the amount of sleep you need. Take a nap every day.

Useful apps and devices to track sleep: Sleep trackers such as the FitBit Charge 2 and the Jawbone UB3 hit the market a couple of years ago, and are a big thing now. They are very helpful in getting you on track with the amount of sleep you're aiming for.

Warning: Please don't use these devices compulsively.

The positive effects of good *sleep* hygiene on productivity, health, and well-being are:

- Cardiovascular health
- Increased energy
- Reduced anxiety levels
- Stress reduction
- Reduced risk of depression
- Cancer prevention
- Reduced inflammation
- Increased focus and alertness
- Improved memory
- Improved weight loss

Whatever Happened to Gloria?

I want to end by giving you some updates on my client Gloria, whom I used as an example earlier in this chapter. After her accident at the airport, and as part of her new program, Gloria got help from her physician who diagnosed her with physical and mental exhaustion. She also underwent a sleep study that showed a mild sleep apnea for which she was treated by wearing a dental device while sleeping. This condition was a culprit to her overall poor health and, by fixing it, she could get some uninterrupted sleep, which improved her quality of life. Gloria's journey to complete recovery was only made possible by honestly reassessing her core beliefs, identifying and connecting to her self-worth, and implementing InnerFitness into her life.

Unfortunately, Gloria's story is one in a billion. I wish for those of you who are suffering from a lack of sleep and a poor quality of life to get the help you need by applying what you are learning in this book. Please let Gloria's story inspire you to take steps toward building a healthy sleep ritual and a healthy life.

CHAPTER TEN

GOLDEN RULE #2: BREATHE

MENTAL CONDITIONING:
CHANGE YOUR BRAIN CHANGE YOUR HABITS

"It's in silence that we find peace and in peace that we find happiness."

1. Meditation
2. Deep breathing
3. Positive visualization
4. Positive affirmations

IN MY PREVIOUS book, *Mind Over Body: The Key to Lasting Weight Loss is All in Your Head!* I outlined a very powerful approach called "The Four Steps from Knowing to Doing." In this approach, I explain that the part of the brain that helps us understand things is not the same part of the brain that helps us apply those things; there is a huge gap between the two. This important information, which the traditional fitness industry either forgot to mention or did not know about at the time, is a must for achieving any kind of goal in life. Needless to say, without proper mental reconditioning, all our efforts will be short-lived. I believe that the lack of a proper mental workout (InnerFitness) and the emphasis on the physical approach (exercise) have been the main obstacle to achieving and maintaining lasting results.

For more than two decades now, my theory has always been one of winning the *inner* game of health and wellness. Therefore, I always recommend a more holistic and mindful approach to working, healthy eating, and exercising.

At the heart of my teachings, I send one powerful message: people should learn how to use their inner power of peak performance if they want to achieve balance in their lives—and that's exactly what you'll learn in this part of the book.

In addition to well-known techniques—such as visualization, which I used to become a world champion—I also recommend mind/body techniques such as meditation, which is generally associated with Eastern spiritual traditions but has not, until now, been applied to teaching true lifelong health and fitness.

In recent years, there has been a lot of media attention surrounding ancient Eastern practices used in fitness, wellness, medicine, and even in business. Practices such as meditation, deep breathing exercises, visualization, and affirmations have been used for thousands of years in the Far East, but are fairly new in Western culture. I have been a longtime user of these techniques and have been prescribing them to my clients worldwide for almost three decades, by combining them with traditional fitness and wellness modalities. Used regularly, these practices will make your results much more effective and long lasting.

Meditation

Meditation is a practice that allows you to relax your body and quiet your conscious mind. It is a way to *not* think. It is one of the most useful tools I know for tapping into the power of the subconscious mind. Practitioners of Eastern religions have long since known this, but recent technological advancements in neuroscience have actually been able to demonstrate visually the positive effects of meditation on the brain.

In terms of general health and fitness, performance, concentration, and focus, meditation is the bridge that connects your body and mind. Without the strength of that connection, I personally would have never been able to feel— mentally and physically—the way I do today. Meditation provides you with a razor-sharp sense of awareness that enables you to identify with the mental, physical, and emotional aspects of your being. By facilitating the amazing and extremely sophisticated relationship between your body and mind, you will enhance the benefits of your workouts and boost performance and productivity. You will be able to listen to the conversation that is taking place between your body and mind, and by that will be mentally prepared to overcome any challenge you encounter in your daily life.

If you've never tried meditation before, now is the time. I think you'll be amazed by how easily your stress melts away as the constant chatter of your conscious mind is silenced and the creative power of the subconscious takes over.

If you've never meditated before, you may feel a bit uncomfortable in the beginning—don't worry. The more you practice, the more comfortable you'll feel. And don't be concerned if you have a hard time "clearing your mind." Thoughts will intrude, and that's okay. Just accept them, and go back to your breathing. You can also use a "mantra," which is a word such as one or the name of a loved one, to help you focus.

Note: Meditation is not something you try or do; it is all about surrendering to the present moment.

There are four simple requirements for practicing meditation:

1. A comfortable position
2. A quiet environment
3. A mental device (such as your mantra)
4. A focused attitude

Four Steps to Meditation for Stress Reducing and Mental Grounding

1. Give yourself permission to stop whatever you're doing and take 10 to 20 minutes when you can be alone and not disturbed. Tell yourself that this time is for your well-being and that you have the right to take it for yourself. You will become more effective and energized if you think of it as your "sacred time alone." I have found that the best time to meditate is right after my morning shower, before I get dressed for the day. But if that time isn't possible for you, just pick one that is.

2. Relax your body by taking a hot bath (if done first thing in the morning or before bedtime), doing some yoga, or doing a deep-breathing exercise. Using aromatherapy will also help, as inhaling the scent will signal neurotransmitters in your brain to produce hormones that calm and soothe the mind. I particularly like, and studies show, that the lavender scent can alleviate anxiety and induce relaxation. Find a quiet spot where you will not be disturbed and sit comfortably on a chair, or on the floor with your legs crossed in front of you. It is better not to lie down, as you don't want to fall asleep during meditation. It may also be helpful if you choose an object to focus on to improve your concentration.

3. Pick any word, sound, short prayer, or phrase upon which to focus. Examples include "peace," "love," "blue," "heal," or simply "one." Close your eyes and, as other thoughts come into your mind (and they will), just let them go and return to your focus word. For instance: "Oh well, Nordine, relax . . . 'one.'" Each time you inhale, imagine that you are breathing in an abundance of health. With each exhale, breathe out the stress and begin to relax every muscle in your body, starting at your feet. Once you feel your feet relax, move on to your ankles, then your calf muscles, and so on, all the way up to your head. Feel your body getting lighter and lighter until you feel yourself floating. Empty your mind of all thought and just concentrate on floating on a soft cloud.

4. When you feel the time you've allotted has passed, simply open your eyes and check your watch or clock (no alarms, please). If the time isn't finished, repeat the process until your 10 to 20 minutes are up. Then take a deep breath, stretch upward and relax your arms, bringing them back down.

Although there are many other forms, this is the most basic for meditation.

The positive effects of *meditation* on productivity, health, and well-being are:

- Enhanced state of awareness
- Increased creativity

- Stress reduction
- Increased performance
- Increased productivity
- Lowered blood pressure
- Reduced levels of anxiety
- Increased ability to focus
- Elevated mood
- Enhanced sleep

For beginners, I personally suggest starting with 20-minute sessions. You can start with as little as five minutes a day, and go from there based on your comfort.

Deep Breathing

Deep Breathing for Instant Stress Release: The Three-Minute Box Breathing Technique

Deep, slow breathing is a powerful tool to release stress and anxiety and find calm. When you have no energy (much less time for your mediation practice) but need to calm yourself down and regain control, deep breathing is the quick answer.

Breathing is at the core of ancient mindfulness practices, from tai chi, qigong, and yoga, to meditation. There are many deep breathing techniques; I personally use "Three-Minute Box Breathing"—relying on this technique to get calm and focused when under tremendous stress—and recommend it to my clients as well. You can practice it anywhere: at your desk, in your parked car, or even in the bathroom.

Find a comfortable place to sit, make sure your back is straight and your feet flat on the floor, and focus all your attention on your breath. Once you've done that, follow these steps:

1. Close your eyes. Let go of all worries and anxieties—just let go!

Breathe in through your nose while counting to three. Feel the air as it goes through your nose and enters your lungs.

2. Hold your breath while counting to three. Try not to clinch your mouth.

3. Exhale for 3 seconds.

4. Hold for 3 seconds.

Repeat steps 1 through 4.

The positive effects of deep breathing on productivity, health, and well-being are:

- An enhanced state of awareness
- An enhanced state of calmness (diffusing conflicts)
- Lowered blood pressure
- Reduced levels of anxiety
- Stress reduction
- Increased energy
- Increased productivity
- Increased ability to focus
- Improved digestion
- Improved immunity

Note: Start with 1 minute and progress to 3 minutes ones or twice a day or as needed.

Visualization

Positive Visualization: If You Want to Have It, You Must First See It!

Visualization is really nothing more than using your inner eye to project an image or series of images on the movie screen of your mind. When we see something in the world around us, that image is sent to and stored in the brain, and the mental images we create for ourselves are stored in the same way. The brain doesn't differentiate between what we see in actuality and what we see in our imagination. The old adage "seeing is believing" holds just as true for mental "seeing" as it does for visual seeing. Whatever outcomes we visualize for ourselves are imprinted on the brain as occurring in actuality. What this means is that we are able to manifest our own destiny.

If you take a few moments at the beginning of each day to visualize yourself completing the tasks you have set for yourself—being at your best, finishing a project, going to the gym, sticking to your diet, etc.—seeing on the screen of your mind how you will do this and how you will look and feel when you've accomplished them will help point you in the right direction. By doing these mental exercises, you'll find that your brain will be using these imprinted images to make your reality match what you've achieved in your imagination.

When I was training for bodybuilding competitions, I used to visualize each part of my body going through my workout routine, seeing my muscles as full and symmetrical, and my form as precise and perfect. Visualizing my workouts before I did them allowed me to imprint these images on my subconscious so that my body would seek to emulate what I had conceived in my mind.

Visualize Your Victory

Visualizing the way you want to look and feel is important for your success in not only physical competition, but life in general. Close your eyes and visualize yourself achieving your desired goals. At first, you may not feel completely comfortable doing this, and the images may not be entirely clear. That's OK, because the more you practice the clearer they will become. Picture the same images every day, adding more detail as you become one with the process. Think of yourself as the lead actor in a movie you are projecting on the screen of your mind. Make sure that when you are doing this, you give an Oscar-winning performance!

During your practice, see yourself feeling refreshed, energized, motivated, and inspired to start your new and successful day. Your mind is so much more powerful than you think. You can overcome any challenge, barrier, and limiting beliefs. Let go of all the ways that have previously held you back. Build new ways of thinking, feeling, responding, and acting. You can be successful, motivated, and inspired.

The positive effects of *positive visualization* on productivity, health, and well-being are:

- Increased self confidence
- Increased clarity
- Increased focus
- Increased performance
- Increased productivity
- Decreased stress
- Increased motivation
- Increased inspiration

Note: I recommend these visual exercises upon arising in the morning and at bedtime.

Affirmations

Positive Affirmations:
The More You Say It, the More You See It!

Affirmations are simple, effective, short, and powerful statements. They allow you to be in conscious control of your thoughts. When you say, think, or even hear them, they become the thoughts that create your reality, helping you move closer to your goals and instantly bridge the gap between mind and body.

Here are a few simple rules to remember when you're creating positive affirmations for yourself.

- Always use the present tense. You want your mind to know that what you affirm has already happened.
- Personalize them by using your name.
- Be absolutely positive. Use as many positive verbs as you can.
- Get emotionally involved with your affirmations by actually *feeling* them.
- Write them down so that you will remember them. Use a journal. Keep them short and specific.
- Repeat them as often as possible in order to imprint what you are affirming.
- Create a habit by setting aside a specific time for doing your affirmations each day.
- Believe that what you say is actually happening. The more you are able to believe, the stronger your affirmation will be.

Repeat each affirmation three times with feeling and trust that, with practice, everything in your life will gently fall into place for your highest good. Take a moment to let go of all your limitations and allow your heart's desires to be created.

Powerful Positive Affirmations

Remember the Affirmations in Chapter Four: Self-Worth?

- I have worth and meaning regardless of my creed, sex, or nationality.
- I seek self-validation.
- I belong to the universe.
- I can do anything.
- I am fearless.

- I know how to sense danger and to protect myself against it.
- I will never look to sabotage myself.
- I know what is in my best interest.
- I know I'm good enough.
- I know how to take criticism and change.
- I know I need to grow and how to grow.

Other Examples

- I have the power to control my health.
- I deserve to be fit now.
- I am ready, willing, and deserve to be wealthy.
- I adopt healthy behaviors.
- I respect and appreciate others.
- I am guided by my true core values.
- I am strong, lean, and beautiful.
- I eat healthy and balanced meals.
- I am losing the unwanted weight surely and smoothly.
- I am strong, intelligent, and attractive.
- I sleep soundly and I feel rejuvenated.
- I am in control of my health and wellness.
- I have abundant energy, vitality, and well-being.
- Health and vitality flow through my veins.
- I am healthy in all aspects of my being.
- I am maintaining my ideal weight.
- I am burning fat easily.
- I am healthy, wealthy, and happy.
- I am fully engaged, focused, and highly productive.

The positive effects of affirmations on productivity, health, and well-being are:

- Increased focus
- Increased clarity

- Increased performance
- Increased productivity
- Increased motivation
- Increased inspiration
- Increased energy

What if I told you that nutrition amounted to 60 percent of the equation for health and well-being? How you eat and what you eat is paramount to success in all aspects of your life. You must fuel both your mind and your body if you want greater vitality and focus to accomplish your goals. Most people neglect this super important part, yet still hope to succeed—that's simply impossible! No wonder they have a hard time implementing most of what they learn through books, seminars, and workshops. That's why the third golden rule is one of the most important.

CHAPTER ELEVEN

GOLDEN RULE #3: EAT
Nutrition For Optimum Performance and Productivity

"Everything you eat will eventually enhance or damage your health. You are what you eat . . . literally!"
- Healthy and Balanced Nutritional Plan
- Hormones

Eat to Live, Not Live to Eat!

OF THE FOUR golden rules, nutrition is perhaps the most important one for general health and well-being. Before going with any kind of nutritional plan, you must first learn about the mental and emotional workings of nutrition.

Why we keep eating the things we know are bad for us?

Why do we keep sabotaging all our efforts after being on a plan for a while?

When people hire me to work with them, most have the same intentions you had when you bought this book. They tell me they want to reduce stress, increase productivity, improve performance, lose weight, get fit, and be happy. But all these intents are not as important as the reason you want this or that. The real question you must ask yourself is "How can I reach long-lasting results?" So I say to my clients that the only way to get meaningful and lasting results is for them to align their thoughts with their self-worth; I put them on a path to aligning body, mind, and spirit so they can achieve and experience perfect work/life balance.

Why Do You Keep Sabotaging All Your Efforts?

Before you embark on a journey to a healthy mind and body, you must identify why you've sabotaged all your efforts in the past—*as you know you have.* What if I told you that the mind is like a computer, in which many beliefs and hidden expectations have been recorded? Those beliefs and expectations have been shaped and guided by our parents, family, teachers, friends, the media, and the Internet, to name a few. So when you're not in sync with your beliefs, you feel anxiety, doubt, and fear.

In my three decades of experience in working with clients worldwide, I've discovered there are two major hurdles to lasting success: the inner image people have of themselves and the inner chatter that keeps feeding those images. This creates a never-ending sabotaging behavior.

It's fair to say that most of you reading this book have at one time sabotaged your efforts to succeed and regain control of your life. You have been driven by a lack of self-worth, stress, fear, doubts, and anxiety that have kept you in a perpetual fight-or-flight response, creating, a negative feedback loop that keeps you unsuccessful, unhealthy, and unhappy.

This fight-or-flight response is a natural event designed to be triggered occasionally. However, and as I've mentioned earlier in this book, career, family, finances, and many other societal expectations all contribute to perpetuating this event. When this becomes persistent, and unmanaged, it can cause stress-related health problems that are exacerbated by the typical Western diet.

> **Warning**: Negative thinking can have strong and sometimes devastating impacts on all aspects of our lives, and can keep us from success and happiness.

Here's an interesting analogy for you: the human mind is like a car that has two engines. One pushes forward (it is our positive aspirations) and the other pulls back (it is our fears, our prejudices and false views, doubts, and guilt). It's not enough that one decides to start meditating, exercising, or eating well; one must commit to a multidimensional assessment.

Lack of performance and weight gain are often consequences of long-held negative chatter, along with some serious stress-related disorders such as depression, insomnia, heart disease, cancer, obesity, high blood pressure, and diabetes.

These conditions and conflicts are all cries for a higher quality of life. Unfortunately, instead of giving ourselves what we really need, we tend to find comfort and solace in foolishness and despair. The obvious problem is that this substitution does not work. If you are not getting the life energy and vitality you need, you will never be able to satisfy your hunger for life.

> "When our lives are lacking or are out of balance, many of us reach for unhealthy behaviors as ways to alleviate or suppress our hunger for life."

It's going to require a dramatically different approach from what's being thrown at you by the mainstream media. But I know we will succeed in working together and bring your life, health, and fitness to their optimum levels.

> **Note**: Happiness is crucial in obtaining long-lasting results; there is simply no way around it. Finding your self-worth and connecting to it will put you right back on the path to success.

Is Your Brain Keeping You Fat and Unhealthy?

Let me say this: your thoughts are not you, and you are not your thoughts. Thoughts are just that—thoughts; they come and they go. If we had to control them all we'd need to be institutionalized. It's simply impossible.

What's more realistic, however, is to not identify or emotionalize your thoughts unless you know they're conducive to your values, self-worth, and goals. As Oprah says: *You become what you believe.* Long-held and repeated thoughts become a manifestation of the object of your thinking. I didn't invent this, I promise! It was already there when you and I came into this world. Many of my clients have been the victims of their own false beliefs. One specific example that comes to mind is my client George, who thought eating one meal a day comprising of a single bagel with everything on it was keeping him healthy and skinny—until it wasn't anymore.

When I started lifting, I knew that I wanted to be a champion. I saw it on the screen of my mind; I fell in love with the idea. There is plenty of research on this topic out there, so I won't bore you with the scientific jargon. My mission, rather, is to give you as many tools as possible so you can be well on your way to success and long-lasting health and wellness.

What Is a Weight Set Point?

The term "set point" is used to describe the weight at which your body likes to be at; it works much like a thermostat (it works the same way in business, too). Your weight set point is determined by several factors, such as heredity and behavior modification. Maybe you've lost 10, 20, or 30 pounds in the past, only to gain it all back after a few months. And just like that, your weight creeps back up to that set number again! Over a long period of time, insufficient exercise and an unhealthy diet will override your body's natural tendency to stay at its set point and lead to a higher, less healthy set point.

> "The mind is a wild stallion; it must be tamed! Only by never wavering and by sticking to your course of action will you able to change your inner identity, set your new body image, and finally experience sustainable and long-lasting results."

So what do you do when that happens? And how can you decrease that number?

Well, you have to start cultivating the right mindset by making a decision to change from the inside out. I promise that by committing to a plan that suits your needs for a sustained period, you will change your set point and be on your way to enjoying your new body identity. Your brain will never fail you again when you match your conscious behaviors with your new and healthier subconscious ones. You will create a perfect harmony between the two. And even if you stumble, you won't give up entirely and will get back on track. When you have the right self-worth and self-image, you'll automatically do what's conducive to your health and well-being. The fitter you'll become, the fitter you'll act. The process will become faster, healthier, and easier than you ever imagined it to be. Success breeds success in any area of life, and healthy eating is no different. When I go out to eat with clients for the first time, they always ask me the same question: "How do you stick to your eating plan?"

My answer is always the same: "My brain knows better! It won't allow me to cheat if it's not my cheat day. I know I'm not supposed to eat certain things, so I won't eat them. Guilt is a very nasty emotion, and I'd rather stick to my plan."

Remember that you've already made your decision to get your life back on a path to optimum health, well-being, and performance, so act decisively on it— dismiss all your doubts and anxiety about it, don't look back, and keep moving forward. Hesitating or reconsidering your new approach will only get you right back to square one.

Fat or Muscles?

People often ask me what my body fat percentage was when I became Mr. Universe. The answer is 3 percent, but that was probably for no more than a couple of days, after which it went back to somewhere between 5 and 7 percent. Assuming you're not a professional bodybuilder, that percentage would be unrealistic.

We all need some fat just to maintain cellular structure, regulate body temperature, cushion and insulate our organs, and store the energy we need simply to stay alive.

The following table indicates the average range of body fat for men and women in various categories.

	WOMEN	MEN
Vital Fat	10-12%	3-5%
Athlete	14-19%	6-13%
Fit	20-24%	14-17%
Average	25-31%	18-25%
Obese	32% or more	26% or more

Note that women naturally have a higher percentage of body fat than

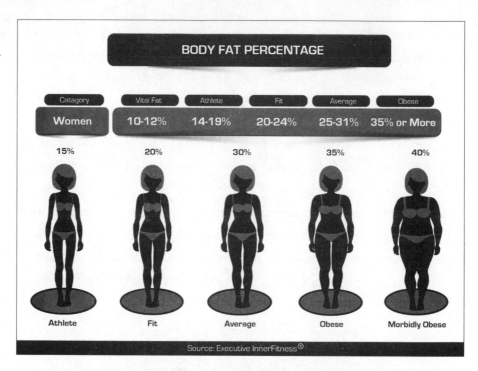

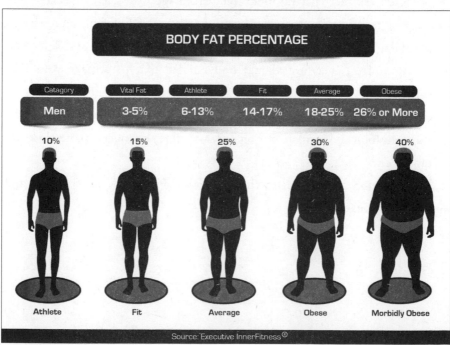

men—about 6 to 7 percent more. By nature, a woman's body is built to protect her potential fetus. As a result, women have more enzymes than men for storing fat and fewer enzymes for burning fat. Furthermore, the estrogen in a woman's system activates fat-storing enzymes and causes them to multiply.

Another difference between men and women is that most women store fat below the waist—in their buttocks, hips, and thighs—whereas most men store it primarily in their abdomen, lower back, and chest. Many studies have shown that the woman's pattern of fat storage is generally healthier than the man's, and that excess abdominal fat indicates an increased risk for developing heart disease.

If You Want to Learn Your Percentage of Body Fat

Although determining your percentage of body fat isn't necessary for following any plan, it can be both interesting and useful before you begin.

You can do this by using calipers designed for such a purpose. If you wish, you can buy the calipers (the Accu-Measure brand costs about fifteen dollars), follow the instructions, and take the measurements yourself. Or—my preference—you can go to a gym and have it done professionally. The American College of Sports Medicine has stated that skinfold measurements, when performed by a trained tester and when using appropriate calipers (i.e,. Lange calipers), are very accurate measures of body fat.

Measuring your body fat before you start a plan and then at intervals as you progress can be very validating and motivating, as you'll see the percentage decline.

My reason for telling you this is to help you understand why it's so important to not only cut calories but also eat a proper balance of nutrients that will help you stay sharp, focused, and build or tone muscle while losing excess weight.

> **Note**: As you increase muscle tone and lose fat, your metabolism will increase, which means that you will begin to burn more calories and therefore lose weight even more quickly. I recommend that you recalculate your calorie requirements every month. One pound of body fat burns 2 to 4 calories a day. One pound of muscle burns 30 to 50 calories a day.

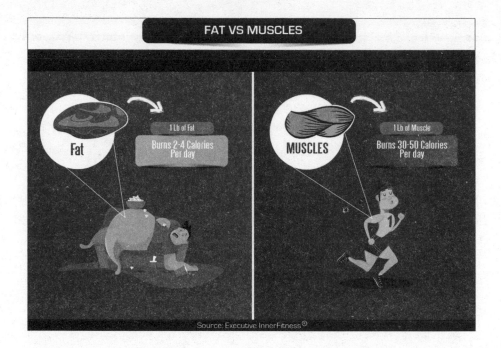

Source: Executive InnerFitness©

Body Mass Index (BMI): Should You Trust It?

Adolphe Quetelet, a Belgian mathematician born in 1796, invented the Body Mass Index (BMI) formula. It was then—and still is now—the favorite and flawed tool to measure a person's healthy weight. Based on the formula, Arnold Schwarzenegger, Sylvester Stallone, and myself are all obese men. Yes, you read it right: *obese*. The formula claims to measure a person's healthy weight by dividing their height by their weight. This formula calculates what's called your BMI score, and then measured on a chart that classifies you as underweight, normal overweight, or obese.

Here's the So-Called Body Mass Index Formula
height in inches ÷ weight in pounds = BMI

The BMI chart is flawed because it doesn't consider muscle mass. Instead, the formula calculates a percentage of your bodyweight, which could be fat or muscle. And while excess body fat mass can show obesity and a slow metabolism, lean muscle mass, in comparison, is an indicator of good health and a faster metabolism. Since both muscle mass and fat weigh about the same, there's no way for the chart to differentiate between the two. A high BMI doesn't mean you're over-weight or have excess body fat. For example, let's take Arnold's weight at his Mr. Universe shape (did he look obese to you?), which was 235 pounds, 6-foot-2, and 7 percent fat percentage. Per the BMI chart, he is still classified as obese.

There are better ways to determine a person's healthy weight. One of my preferred methods is by measuring your waistline—it tells you everything. It's always best to get a clear picture of your body composition, rather than trusting a number that makes a rather vague statement about one's health.

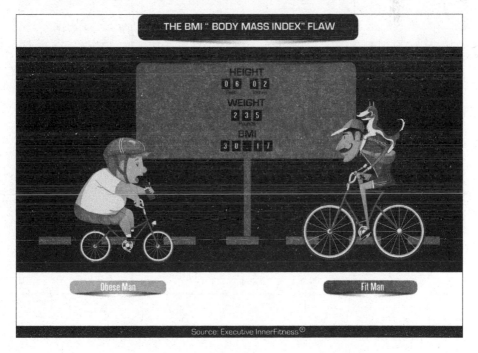

Determine Your "Ideal" Weight

Before you start any fat-loss journey, you'll need to know where you want to end up. Please note that I've put the word *ideal* in quotation marks. That's because I don't want you to think of it as the weight you *must* aim to reach. The following charts were created by the Metropolitan Life Insurance Company based on statistics associated with the lowest risk of mortality. However, each one of us is unique; no two of us have exactly the same bone structure or body composition, and some of us have particular health issues or other concerns that need to be taken into account. Therefore, consider what weight will make you feel

♀ Ideal Height and Weight Chart for Women			
Height ⊥	Small Frame	Medium Frame	Large Frame
4 10	102-111	109-121	118-131
4 11	103-113	111-123	120-134
5 0	104-115	113-126	122-137
5 1	106-118	115-129	125-140
5 2	108-121	118-132	128-143
5 3	111-124	121-135	131-147
5 4	114-127	124-138	134-151
5 5	117-130	127-141	137-155
5 6	120-133	130-144	140-159
5 7	123-136	133-147	143-163
5 8	126-139	136-150	146-167
5 9	129-142	139-153	149-170
5 10	132-145	142-156	152-173
5 11	135-148	145-159	155-176
6 0	138-151	148-162	158-179

comfortable and fit. You also need to be realistic. If you haven't weighed at the low end of the range for your height since you hit puberty, that target is probably unrealistic. Don't set yourself up for failure by setting a goal your body isn't capable of achieving.

Weights at ages twenty-five to fifty-nine, based on lowest mortality. Weight in pounds according to frame (in indoor clothing weighing three pounds; shoes with one-inch heels).

Reprinted with the permission of MetLife, this information is not intended to be a substitute for professional medical advice and should not be regarded as an endorsement or approval of any product or service.

♂ Ideal Height and Weight Chart for Men			
Height	Small Frame	Medium Frame	Large Frame
5 2	128-134	131-141	138-150
5 3	130-136	133-143	140-153
5 4	132-138	135-145	142-156
5 5	134-140	137-148	144-160
5 6	136-142	139-151	146-164
5 7	138-145	142-154	149-168
5 8	140-148	145-157	152-172
5 9	142-151	148-160	155-176
5 10	144-154	151-163	158-180
5 11	146-157	154-166	161-184
6 0	149-160	157-170	164-188
6 1	152-164	160-174	168-192
6 2	155-168	164-178	172-197
6 3	158-172	167-182	176-202
6 4	162-176	171-187	181-207

Weights at ages twenty-five to fifty-nine, based on lowest mortality. Weight in pounds according to frame (in indoor clothing weighing three pounds; shoes with one-inch heels).

Reprinted with the permission of MetLife, this information is not intended to be a substitute for professional medical advice and should not be regarded as an endorsement or approval of any product.

The size of your frame is based on the circumference of your wrist in relation to your height. Measure your wrist with a tape measure and use the following chart to determine the size of your frame.

Frame Size Women
Height under 5-foot-2
Small = Wrist < 5.5"
Medium = Wrist 5.5" to 5.75"
Large = Wrist > 5.75"
Height under 5-foot-2
Small = Wrist < 6"
Medium = Wrist 6" to 6.25"
Large = > 6.25"
Height over 5-foot-5
Small = Wrist < 6.25"
Medium = Wrist 6.25" to 6.5"
Large = Wrist > 6.5"

Frame Size Men
Height over 5-foot-5
Small = Wrist 5.5" to 6.5"
Medium = Wrist 6.5" to 7.5"
Large = Wrist > 7.5"

Now, you have a target to shoot for.

Become Conscious of What You're Thinking

Since I'm all about using your mind to change your body and your life, I suggest that, before you go any further, you check in with your subconscious to see whether you still harbor any of the following beliefs. To make sure that you're really focused and in touch with your thoughts, do the following deep-breathing exercise:

- Inhale deeply and hold the breath in for 3 seconds; exhale and repeat this process three times.
- Make yourself comfortable.
- Roll your neck gently forward and to the left side, then forward again and to the right side—not backwards, which will put pressure on the back of the neck. Repeat this 10 times. Breathe through your nose, inhaling as you move your head to the right and exhaling as you move it to the left. Repeat this exercise five times to each side.

Now, consider which of the following statements reflect your own beliefs.

- I feel tired; I need food.

- I know everything about exercising and eating healthy; I'll start next week.
- I love food too much; I'll never be able to stick with this diet.
- I have tried before and failed every time; I am not strong enough mentally.
- I will never be able to concentrate on my work if I have to starve every day.
- My husband (or my wife, or my partner) cooks so well, I can't resist.
- We always go out to eat; it's impossible to diet when you're eating in restaurants.
- Weekends are times to eat.
- I'll start my diet Monday.
- I am stressed and it makes me eat more.
- If I eat more today, I'll workout more tomorrow.
- I love my beer too much after dinner, when I'm sitting in front of the TV.
- No way I will give up ice cream after dinner.
- I travel for my job, and I have to stay in hotels and eat what's available.
- I am overweight, but I am happy; why would I change who I am?

Once you become aware of these thoughts, they'll help you understand how they are causing you to behave.

Disconnect Your Food from Your Emotions

We've all heard about comfort foods, but they are only so because we associate them with happy memories. Subconsciously, when we are feeling sad or stressed, we crave the foods that we connect with feeling happy.

Ellen, a client of mine, once told me, "Dinner was the only time for our family to be together. All day we were busy, and every night we rejoiced with food. With each mouthful and each chew, I was enjoying my family time. I wanted it to last forever, so I went on eating and eating." By bringing that memory to consciousness, Ellen was able to understand that it was really the happy memory of spending time with her family that she cherished, not the food itself.

Think about the foods that "trigger" you to overeat. It may well be that they are precisely the foods you connect with particularly pleasurable moments from your past. If you focus on remembering what those moments were, you'll be able to disconnect the emotion from the food and become more mindful of why and what you are eating. Doing a meditation to clear and focus your mind will help you to bring those subconscious associations to consciousness.

How to Think about Any Healthy Nutritional Plan

The best piece of advice I can give you is not to think of your nutritional plan as a diet. A diet is something people go "on" to lose weight and then "off." They then gain the weight back and go "on" the diet again. You've probably done that yourself at least a few times in the past. I, too, have been on diets.

When I was a professional bodybuilder, I did some crazy and sometimes unsafe things to my body in order to compete. One of the dumbest things I ever did was when, at the age of twenty-one, I stopped drinking water for 72 hours before a competition so that I would look super lean—or, as we say in the body-building world, "ripped." Why would I do such a thing? Because one of my teammates suggested it! I would have wound up in the hospital instead of on stage if my own instincts—not to mention the fact that I appeared to be shrink-ing by the minute and was feeling horrible—hadn't told me to drink. Within hours I was back to normal. I didn't win the competition (I did come in sec-ond), but I learned a valuable lesson.

I haven't done anything that crazy since, and haven't "dieted" since my last competition, "The Night of Champions," in 1991. Since then, I've been follow-ing a balanced, healthy, nutritional plan very similar to the one I'll be giving you. It's a way to eat for the rest of your life.

> "Excess weight or weight gain is not actually the problem; it's a symptom of the underlying problem, which is the accumulation of unhealthy body fat. And the cause of excess body fat is the lack of muscle. Therefore, you must concentrate on building muscle and losing fat—forever."

In addition to the on-again, off-again nature of diets, they can also be both physically and emotionally harmful. Many diets are so restrictive that they cause you to lose muscle mass and slow your metabolism, actually encouraging your body to store fat instead of burning it. In addition, they can create vitamin and mineral deficiencies that leave you fatigued and craving the very starchy, sugary foods you should be avoiding.

Very often, people who come to consult with me say that they're 30 pounds overweight. I look at them and tell them they're wrong. In actuality, they're probably carrying 40 pounds of excess fat and lacking 30 pounds of muscle. When I suggest this, most people are surprised—they never thought of the various kinds of tissue that contribute to their total bodyweight.

As many of us know, a pound of fat has more than twice the volume of a pound of muscle. But think about what this actually means. By changing the ratio of muscle to fat in your body, you'll actually weigh more but look thinner. If, for example, you weigh 135 pounds but have only 24 pounds of body fat, you'll easily fit into clothing that someone who is the same weight but has 40 pounds of body fat couldn't possibly wear.

In addition to how you look, however, your ratio of muscle to fat can also have a profound impact on your overall health and fitness. In fact, many of the health issues associated with excess body fat—chronic fatigue syndrome, lower back pain, high blood pressure, and high cholesterol, just to name a few—actually result from a loss of muscle.

I. Healthy and Balanced Nutritional Plan

As I've mentioned at the beginning of this chapter, nutrition is perhaps the most important one. The problem people have is that they often follow diets that don't work. Most fad diets are not sustainable and are potentially dangerous to one's health and well-being. I see it all the time. People will do anything to lose weight—including risking their health.

Except for a few exceptions—such as my Bedouin grandpa, Ali, who lived near the Sahara Desert and survived on freshly made organic bread, hot peppers, coffee, and milk—it's always best to eat healthy and balanced meals for optimum performance.

My all-time favorite nutritional plan—and the one I recommend to most of my clients—is the 40/40/20 x 5. The diet consists of 40 percent carbohydrates,

40 percent protein, 20 percent fats, times five meals a day. On this plan, you won't have to eat any specific foods at any specific time. You'll always have plenty to choose from, so you won't be bored and will be able to eat out and enjoy your meals without worrying about going off the plan. This plan is easy and most accommodating.

For those who need to bring their weight down to a healthy and safe level, you should expect to reduce anywhere between one to three pounds a week. You'll have an amazing and sustained energy that will last throughout the day. This plan will get you lean, fit, mentally sharp, and recharged.

If this plan works for you, it will be a permanent way of eating for life.

It's really as simple as 1, 2, 3.

1. For every meal, think 40/40/20.

Forty percent of your diet should consist of carbohydrates that are low to moderate on the glycemic index (those that are absorbed more slowly and therefore do not spike blood sugar levels), 40 percent of proteins of high biological value (those that are most easily digested, are quickly absorbed by the cells, and most closely match the types of protein found in the body), and 20 percent of heart-healthy fats.

2. Stick to correct portion sizes.

A "portion" for most of us is a lot of food we are accustomed to being served, particularly in restaurants. See "nature's way" method below.

3. Eat five small meals a day, at three-hour intervals.

By doing this, you'll ensure that you're never "starving" and that your blood sugar is steady throughout the day. As a result, you won't be tempted to overeat or grab the first fatty, sugary snack that crosses your path.

If you follow these three simple rules, you can expect to have a steady source of energy from morning to night, your brain will be sharp, and your body will be strong.

Use Nature's Way to Determine Portion Size

Luckily, nature has provided a very easy way for you to determine the correct portion size without having to weigh or measure anything.

- A portion of carbohydrate is the size of your fist.
- A portion of protein is the size of your palm.
- A portion of fat is the length of your thumb from the first joint to the tip.

Why does this work? Because the bigger you are, the bigger your palm and fist are. The size of your body is telling you the size of the portion you should be eating.

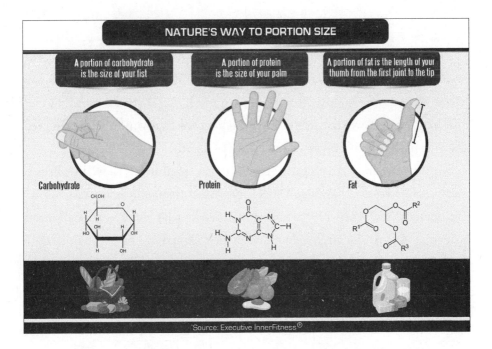

NATURE'S WAY TO PORTION SIZE

A portion of carbohydrate is the size of your fist

A portion of protein is the size of your palm

A portion of fat is the length of your thumb from the first joint to the tip

Carbohydrate

Protein

Fat

Source: Executive InnerFitness©

How to Avoid Portion Distortion

Unfortunately, most Americans are so used to "supersizing" everything that they no longer have any idea what a proper portion should look like. Portion sizes in fast-food restaurants are now three to four times larger than they were in the 1950s. This means that, at least initially, you may be worried that with this plan you're not going to be getting enough food to fill you up. In fact, because you're eating every three hours, you really don't have to be concerned about going hungry. But if you want to be on the safe side, you can fill your plate with "free" vegetables. No one ever got fat from eating vegetables!

If you're worried about overeating, determine the correct portion size before you cook your food, and don't prepare any extra—if it isn't there in front of you, you won't be tempted to eat it. Or you can meal prep, which allows you to eat your portion without worrying about consuming too much food. This method is particularly helpful if you don't have the time to cook each day and find yourself eating out as a result.

You can also fool the eye—and your mind—by using small plates. If your plate is full, portions will appear more generous.

Why Eat Five Times a Day?

The most important reason to eat frequent smaller meals is that you'll always be eating before you're ravenously hungry, which will make it much easier for you to control the amount you consume at each meal. You'll also be ensuring that your blood sugar level remains stable, which means that you won't be tempted to rev yourself up with sugary, starchy, high-GI carbs.

But there are important health reasons to eat small meals as well. A British study conducted at Cambridge University ("Meal frequency and plasma lipids and lipoproteins," April 1997) showed that people who ate several small meals instead of one or two large ones reduced their cholesterol by approximately 5 percent, even when they ate more total calories and more calories from fat than when they were eating larger meals. "Total cholesterol and low-density lipoprotein ["bad" LDL cholesterol] decreased in a continuous relation with increasing daily frequency of eating," states the report published in the *British Medical Journal*. "This finding was particularly striking in view of the increased [caloric] intake, including fat intake, in people who reported eating more frequently."

Of course, you must take in consideration that the extra food eaten should still be of a high quality that will not disrupt your immune system and impair your insulin balance.

Another good reason to eat small meals is that when you take in calories from food, your body either uses them for energy or stores them as fat. So if you eat too many calories at a single meal and don't expend them as energy, guess what happens? Those "extra" calories get stored as fat. So if you're concerned about weight loss, it makes sense not to eat more calories than you expend in any given period of time. Realistically, you probably won't be eating *exactly* the same number of calories at every meal, but it would be best if you tried to keep your meals as equal as possible. Most of you may be used to thinking of the mid-morning and mid-afternoon meals as snacks. These may be as simple as a protein shake or bar, or a small meal such as cottage cheese and nuts, but I call them meals because they should provide approximately the same number of calories as the other meals and should contain protein and carbohydrates, as well as a small amount of good fat. Think of your snacks as convenient, energizing meal replacements.

If you want to have a protein bar as a snack, make sure you read the label carefully. There are many brands of protein bars available, so try a few different ones until you find those you like best. You should be looking for those that contain no more than 8 grams of sugar and 8 grams of fat.

Preparation for Convenience

If you are using inconvenience as an excuse for not taking your meals with you to the office, here is an idea: meal prep (as I mentioned earlier). Get yourself one of those "meal management backpacks, or bags. They are very convenient, and you can find them at any supplements store or online. Prep all your meals for the day or week.

Why the Plan Works

- The "good" carbs will stabilize your blood sugar and insulin levels so that you no longer crave sugary, starchy carbs.
- The protein will fill you up and keep you feeling fuller longer so that you aren't tempted to overeat at your next meal. Protein also helps to build the muscle that will boost your metabolism so that you burn your calories faster.

- Your body is extremely efficient about turning the fat you eat into body fat. It takes much more energy to convert carbohydrates into fat. Reducing your fat intake will mean that your body is burning the fat you already have as your primary source of energy.
- Eating five times a day means that you'll be consuming fewer calories at each meal.
- You'll never be hungry, so you won't be tempted to overeat. In fact, if you eat more than the recommended amounts, you'll find that you feel stuffed and uncomfortable.

Mindful Hunger

Your body is your baby; nurture it and feed it when it cries. If you're a parent, you undoubtedly know that a baby cries when it's hungry. You wouldn't ignore your baby's cry for food, and you shouldn't ignore yours.

This plan asks you to eat five times a day—or approximately every three hours—because the surest way to overeat is to wait until you're absolutely famished. If you wait until you're "starving," you'll be gulping your food down and could easily eat up to 5,000 calories before your brain has a chance to let your stomach know it's full. Use your mind to help your body by being aware of how hungry you are and eat when you're at a two or three on the scale below.

1_____	2_____	3_____	4_____	**5 HOURS**
Not Hungry	Moderately Hungry	Hungry	Very Hungry	Starving

Don't eat when you're not hungry, and don't wait until you're very hungry or starving.

How Hungry Are You?

People on restrictive diets often feel hungry all the time because they've disconnected the mechanism by which the brain signals the body that it's full. As a result, they will start eating because they're really stressed or upset, not because they're hungry. Here are a few tips for getting back in touch with your hunger signals.

- It takes 20 minutes from the time you start eating for the brain to signal the stomach that you're full. So, if you eat too quickly, you'll have overstuffed yourself before that signal has time to arrive. Eat slowly and be mindful of what you're your brain is telling your body.
- If you think you're hungry, drink a glass of water and wait approximately 15 minutes to see if you still feel hunger. If you drink a full glass of water before you begin each meal, you won't be confusing hunger with thirst.
- If you think you're hungry, try engaging in an activity you enjoy. You may discover that you were only thinking about food because you were bored, stressed, fatigued, or frustrated with what you were doing.
- If you're craving something sweet, wait 15 minutes. Involve yourself in an activity or engage in conversation, and more often than not your craving will pass. If you still crave sweets after 15 minutes, try eating a healthier alternative, such as sugar-free frozen yogurt. Or eat just a small amount of the food you crave.

How Much Protein Do You Need, and When?

If you are not a bodybuilder and you're in the "most people" category, you need 0.4 grams of protein per pound of bodyweight to meet your basic protein daily requirements. If you exercise, however, you may need additional protein. The most important thing is to consume between 20 to 45 grams of protein (muscle building) every three to four hours max. Most of your protein daily requirements should come from lean beef, egg whites, fish or chicken, or various food combinations if you are vegetarian or a vegan. But for the sake of practicality or convenience, if you are consuming five or more meals a day—as it is the case with the 40/40/20 x 5 nutritional plan—you should consume up to 35 percent of your protein requirement from protein powder (that's about two shakes a day). Some weight loss plans recommend taking more protein powder (as meal replacements) for a short period (seven days). I recommend that you consult with a healthcare professional if you are thinking of going on such a plan.

The following recommendations are based on the assumption that you are using only 35 percent of your required protein intake as protein powder supplements and 65 percent in solid foods such as lean beef, eggs, fish, chicken, quinoa, and other food combos if you are a vegetarian or a vegan.

Adults:

Most People: 0.4 gram per lb./bodyweight
Endurance Training: 0.5-0.8 gram per lb./bodyweight
Strength/Muscle Building: 0.8-1 gram per lb./bodyweight

Recommended Dietary Allowances (RDA) for Teenagers:

13 year old: 35 grams/day
14-18 (girls): 46 grams/day
14-18 (boys): 52 grams/day
Teen athletes: 0.5-0.8 grams per lb./bodyweight

Note: Drink one or two whey protein shakes with the recommended amount a day or as prescribed by a healthcare professional. Choose high quality 100 percent natural, grass-fed isolate whey protein powder with no hormones, no antibiotics, no chemicals and GMOs. Never replace all your solid food with meal replacement supplements. If you are vegan, I suggest you use plant-based protein powder.

The positive effects of eating balanced and healthy meals on productivity, health, and well-being are:

- Getting and staying healthy
- Increased weight loss
- Increased muscle tone (combined with exercise)
- Stabilized blood sugar

- Stopping sugar cravings
- Increased and sustained energy levels
- Lowered cortisol (stress hormone) levels
- Increased metabolism
- Increased sleep quality

I recommend that you find a nutritional plan that fits your lifestyle, one that's sustainable and that you can use long term. The 40/40/20 x 5 is such a plan.

II. Hormones: Balancing Your Hormones for Health, Energy, and Vitality

"Whenever we feel stressed out, that's a signal that our brain is pumping out stress hormones. If sustained over months and years, those hormones can ruin our health and make us a nervous wreck."

—Daniel Goleman, author and science journalist

Are These Hormones Making You Fat and Miserable?

Balancing your hormones is key to your health, energy, and vitality. Without a perfect balance, your performance will suffer. Herein are seven essential hormones involved in making you feel well, enhance fat burning, increase muscle tone, and enhance your overall mood.

1. Insulin

Insulin regulates the metabolism of carbohydrates and fats and is key for muscle building, recovering from exercise, and maintaining optimal blood sugar levels. The more you eat simple carbohydrates or sugar, the more insulin will be released. When more insulin is released, it can inhibit the breakdown and burning of stored fat.

Solution: Eating low-to-moderate glycemic index carbs will help optimize insulin. The 40/40/20 x 5 nutritional plan (or any healthy and balanced nutritional plan) can help with avoiding insulin spikes, maintain blood sugar levels, and promoting fat burning.

2. Leptin

Leptin is a hormone that plays an important role in appetite and weight control. It is released exclusively from fat cells. Leptin has been called the "starvation hormone," as it tells your brain to get your body to eat less and burn more calories. The more body fat you have, the more leptin your fat cells will release—though, too much body fat leads to too much leptin being released—a condition called leptin resistance. When this happens, your brain doesn't respond to leptin's signal.

Solution: Make sure you are sleeping seven to nine hours a night. Finish your last meal at 8 p.m. and resume eating twelve hours later (the next day).

3. Glucagon

Glucagon is the opposite of insulin. Its main job in the body is to raise the blood sugar level when it is too low. Glucagon is responsible for breaking down stored carbohydrates and fats, releasing them for your body to fuel itself. When glucagon levels rise too high—usually because of undereating—muscle loss is experienced.

Solution: Eating a protein-rich, low-to-moderate glycemic index carbohydrate meals is the best way to maximize glucagon release. The 40/40/20 x 5 nutritional plan (or any healthy and balance nutritional plan) can help create balance between glucagon and insulin levels.

4. Ghrelin

Ghrelin is your "Hunger Hormone." It is produced in your stomach and tells your brain to signal that you are hungry. Eating a low-calorie diet causes an increase in ghrelin. Getting less than seven to eight hours' sleep will also cause an increase in ghrelin. If you want to lose weight, you want less ghrelin.

Solution: Sleep seven to nine hours a night. Exercising will also help you decrease ghrelin levels, making it a key element to fat loss and weight maintenance.

5. Cholecystokinin (CCK)

CKK is a peptide hormone of the gastrointestinal system responsible for stimulating the digestion of fat and protein. It tells your nervous system to start the satiety process while simultaneously working with your stomach to slow the rate of digestion, therefore making you feel fuller longer.

Solution: Making sure you have high biological value (BV) protein and good fat at every meal will ensure that you're taking advantage of this hormone. The 40/40/20 x 5 nutritional plan (or any healthy and balance nutritional plan) can help to accommodate that.

6. Growth Hormone

Considered to be the "miracle hormone," growth hormone helps in increasing lean body mass, decreasing body fat, increasing effectiveness of the immune system, increasing memory, libido, and stamina. Low levels of human growth hormone (HGH) can cause low energy levels, increased body fat, anxiety, depression, and the weakening of the immune system.

Solution: Growth hormone can be increased by using the exercises outlined in this book. To maximize the fat-burning effect of growth hormone, train smart, eat healthy, and get plenty of sleep.

7. Cortisol

Cortisol is produced by the adrenal glands; two peanut-shaped glands that sit just above the kidneys, deep in the abdominal cavity. Cortisol is a hormone that is needed by the body for normal immune system function, regulation of blood pressure, and regulation of inflammation. High levels of cortisol are known to be a cause of decreased bone density, increased blood pressure, suppression of the immune system, muscle wasting, insulin resistance, and certainly a main cause of increased body fat levels. In additional to stress, there are additional factors that can elevate cortisol, including significant fluctuation in blood sugar, excessive carbohydrates relative to your needs, protein deficiencies, and even eating too little can cause cortisol to rise.

Cortisol is able to overpower just about all hormones in the body. It will raise glucose even when insulin is trying to lower it. Cortisol can lower glucose in the presence of glucagon. It can cause the accumulation of body fat—even if you're doing just about everything correctly. Cortisol will also block HGH from doing its job.

Solution: The proper level of cortisol is achieved through a proper combination of food, meditation and relaxation techniques such as breathing exercises. By mixing the right amounts of the right foods at the right time, you can bring about an optimal level of cortisol.

Note that if you are a woman entering your menopausal years, it's always a good idea to have a comprehensive hormone panel ordered to check if you are maintaining a healthy balance. Men could also benefit by checking their hormones, especially after age fifty. You can ask your doctor to prescribe a comprehensive hormonal panel. Once you receive your lab results, your doctor will be able to read them back to you and assess the proper course of action. In most cases they will recommend that you relax more, exercise, eat healthy and balanced meals and sleep better. Always be prepared to ask about natural available therapy options.

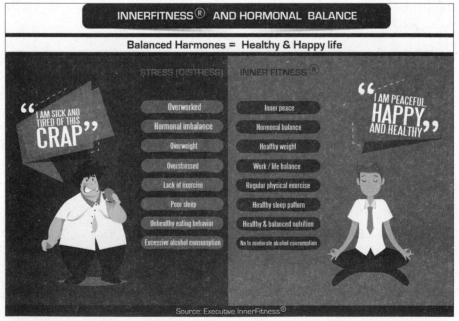

A picture is worth a thousand words indeed!

CHAPTER TWELVE

GOLDEN RULE #4: MOVE

EXERCISE YOUR WAY TO SUCCESS: THE THIRTY-MINUTE STRESS AND ANXIETY BUSTER WORKOUT PLAN

If you look in the mirror and you don't want the body you see, you will actually be attracting more of what you don't want. If you want a great body, you need to think about having a great body.

EXERCISE IS A powerful tool in preventing or reducing stress and anxiety. People who exercise five times a week for at least 30 minutes are 25 percent less likely to develop anxiety than those who do not. In cases of mild anxiety, exercise can be helpful, easing symptoms in as little as a few minutes. Although exercise and nutrition are paramount to good health, obsessing over them can signal unhealthy behaviors. In my experience working with clients, I've seen cases of body obsessions, fitness obsessions, weight obsessions, excessive exercise, anorexia, bulimia, and binge-eating disorders.

These unhealthy behaviors develop when exercise or nutrition is used to extreme limits. With over-exercising and fitness obsession, the likely effects can include injuries, exhaustion, anxiety, depression, and total isolation.

As Oscar Wilde said: "Everything in moderation, even moderation itself!"

Part of my coaching clients is making sure they aren't obsessed on a particular exercise modality three hours a day, seven days a week. Go to any large gym and you'll find the cardio machines occupied by people who are there when you begin your workout and are still there when you finish. What I am teaching you in Rule #4: Move, is spending hours on the cross trainer, treadmill, or stair-climber will never get you in shape. You need to do a combination of strength, flexibility, and cardiovascular training, for a reasonable amount of time, and your strength training always needs to precede the cardio segment of your workout if done during the same session.

The positive effects of exercising on productivity, health, and well-being are:

- Increased metabolism
- Cardiovascular health
- Increased energy
- Reduced anxiety levels
- Reduced stress
- Reduced risk of depression
- Reduced inflammation
- Improved memory
- Weight loss
- Increased muscle tone
- Enhanced sleep quality
- Reduced pain
- Improved sex life

> **Note**: I recommend you exercise at least 30 minutes, three to five days a week.

Shift Your Perspective on Fitness

Before going over the different recommended exercise modalities, I'm asking you to consider fitness from a new perspective. Instead of mere body consciousness, approach fitness from the point of view of *mind* and *body* consciousness. This is an important aspect of mindful fitness.

If you go to the gym and turn off your brain while your body performs a routine, you'll be gaining only half the benefit of what you're doing. Being aware of where you are and what you're doing at every moment means that you are not only concentrating on the exercise being performed, but also remembering the purpose of why you're doing it. By remaining mindful, your routine will not simply be goal-ori-

"Live every minute as if it were your last. Perform every movement and every set of every exercise as if it were your last."

ented but process-oriented; in other words, you'll be moving from "doing" to "being." You will be observing each moment.

That said, the most important thing you can do for your body—as you exercise—is to keep your mind present and focused. Since your body takes its instruction from your mind, a lack of focus results in a lack of effectiveness.

Why Longer Isn't Better

Cortisol is used by the body to break down muscle protein into amino acids for energy. Cortisol levels begin to rise after about an hour of training. Since you don't want to break down muscle tissue or stress your body by raising your cortisol levels, **you shouldn't work out for more than an hour at a time.**

In addition, a 2011 study in the *Journal of Obesity* has shown that working at greater intensity for a shorter period of time is more beneficial for fat loss than working longer at lower intensity.

The purpose of the "30-Minute Stress and Anxiety Buster Workout Plan" is to keep yourself moving by taking short breaks between exercises, which will increase oxygen to the brain and release mood-enhancing and stress-reducing endorphins. You'll be working your body aerobically while still challenging your strength, which will maximize fat loss and increase your muscle tone, making you feel (mind) and look (body) good. You could spend a lot more time in the gym chatting and socializing, but that would only make your workout less rather than more effective.

Seek Quality, Not Quantity

One of the first questions clients always ask me is, "How much is enough?" And my answer is always the same: "Spending more time working out is not necessarily better." The key is to do the right routine with the right amount of focus and intensity. That ought to be great news if you've been using the top excuse for not exercising, which is—that's right—"I don't have enough time!"

How Does It Work?

Like my nutrition plan, it's as easy as 1, 2, 3!

- Do 15 minutes of upper body strength training (chest, back, shoulders, triceps, biceps, upper abs, and waist) followed by 15 minutes of cardio interval training on days one and four.
- On the third day, do 30 minutes of cardio interval training only.
- Do 15 minutes of lower-body strength training (quads, glutes, hamstrings, adductors, abductors, calves, lower abs, and waist) followed by 15 minutes of cardio interval training on days two and five.

1: Strength Training

What You Need to Know about Strength Training?

Simply put, strength training means working out with weights or machines that offer resistance in order to strengthen and build your bones and muscles. This is possibly the single most important thing you can do to improve your overall health and increase longevity.

After the age of thirty, everyone starts to lose both bone and muscle mass.

Strength training can help to rebuild lost bone and, thus, decrease the risk for osteoporosis, which strikes half of all women after the age of fifty and can affect men as well (and can also be the culprit for developing mental health issue). In addition, the American College of Sports Medicine has found that lean muscle mass decreases by almost 50 percent between the ages of twenty and ninety. And, whenever we lose lean muscle, we replace it with fat.

That said, strength training will not only help to keep you healthy (both mentally and physically), but will also help you to lose weight. One reason for this, as I've said, is that muscle burns more calories than fat; so the more muscle you build, the faster you'll burn. But there's more.

Recent research at Colorado State University indicates that after you've

Throughout my entire career as a pro athlete, I never worked my body for more than an hour a day, and even then I split my workout into two 30-minute sessions. The program I'm offering you here requires only 30 minutes a day, five days a week, of focused and effective exercise.

completed a strength-training or cardio workout, your metabolism remains elevated for several hours, which means, of course, that you're burning more calories not only during your workout, but for a long time after you finish. This is known as excess post-exercise oxygen consumption, or EPOC. The study suggests that there's a link between the number of calories burned post exercise and the activity's intensity. In other words, the more intense the workout, the more oxygen your body consumes afterward. You'd still be burning calories at the office.

Any strength-training program should target all the major muscle groups in the legs, chest, back, shoulders, arms, and—especially for women—the core muscles in the abdomen and lower back. Strengthening the abdomen and lower back helps to increase bone density in the hips and promote good posture, which makes it easier to perform the activities of daily life with more strength and better balance.

Strength Training Always Comes First

You may be wondering why strength training always comes before your cardio training. That's because to achieve maximum results, you need to have your greatest strength and energy to do your strength training. In addition, the strength training will empty your glycogen stores (the storage form of glucose) so that you begin to burn fat more quickly when you start your cardio exercise.

Which Type of Strength Training?

There are many options when it comes to strength training, and sometimes it can be overwhelming to find the type that fits your age, lifestyle, needs, and limitations. Here is a list of effective and safe strength training options I usually recommend:

- Resistance machines (home or gym)
- Free weights (home or gym)
- Strength classes (gym)
- Kettlebells (home or gym)
- Resistance bands (home)
- Calisthenics exercises (home)
- Medicine balls (home)
- Pilates (home or gym)

Ultimately, the most effective exercise modality—and the one you'll be more likely to adhere to—is the one you'll have the most fun with.

Free Weights or Machines—Which Way Is Better?

I'm certainly not against using machines for strength training. In fact, I continue to use them as part of my own strength-training workout. That said, for most people who are not professional athletes, free weights are more functional and compatible with the tasks we perform on a daily basis. Groceries, books, furniture, home-care tools, and children—in other words, the things we lift and move in the course of daily life—are not fixed weights that move in only one direction. We pick up and move these items without the benefit of guides, rails, and levers. Therefore, we need to train our bodies to move in multiple planes and angles to comply with real-life movements. Free weights—dumbbells, medicine balls, and ankle weights—are better training tools than machines for everyday life, not only because they mimic our most common movements but also because they help us develop better balance and strengthen the muscles of the torso that stabilize the spine and provide a solid foundation for movement in the extremities.

In addition, during the first four to six weeks of strength training, you're increasing muscular coordination and sensory awareness—both of which develop less quickly if you use machines that work in only one plane of motion.

So even if you decide to use machines, I recommend that you begin your training with free weights.

For cardiovascular training, unless you live in a climate where you can engage in outdoor activities year-round, machines will make your exercise routine a lot easier and more convenient. They also add variety, which may help to keep you challenged and interested.

My personal favorite is the cross-trainer, as it provides a workout for both your upper and lower body all at once. I also like the elliptical trainer and the treadmill, both of which work you hard and provide a good lower-body workout. Stationary bikes and stair climbers don't work you as hard, but, of course, this is all relative and you can certainly get a good workout on a stationary bike set at high intensity than you would with a cross-trainer at low intensity. Cross-trainers and ellipticals also put less stress on your joints than, for example, a treadmill, as they are non-impact machines. The bottom line is to use the machine that best fits your needs and capabilities, so pick the one you like best or change things up (if that's what keeps you going).

Before You Begin Strength Training—
Gauge Your Level of Intensity

You should be able to perform at least 12 repetitions of each exercise with the last three requiring a challenging effort. If you can't do 12, you may be using too much weight. If you can do more than 15 without feeling challenged, the weight is probably too light. Test yourself and adjust your weight accordingly.

Your strength may begin to improve after just three to four weeks of consistent training. When you no longer feel that your sets are challenging enough, you will need to increase the amount of weight you are using in order to continue those gains.

Believe it or not, soreness—along with boredom and lack of results—are some reasons people find it hard to stick to their exercise program. Intimidation, fear of not measuring up to others at the gym, fear of not being firm enough, fit enough, attractive enough—these are all limiting beliefs most people have when first starting to workout at a gym. When I started, I was so shy that I waited for the gym to be almost empty before beginning my workout. I felt intimidated by

the big guys. They looked too good for me to even
fathom about having a body like that. I know now
that the lack of self-worth was the culprit for my
behavior. Then I got comfortable and understood
that I wasn't there to be better, bigger, or fitter
than anyone else. It is then that I showed signs of
self-confidence. If you experience those feelings,
stop and remember that you are already enough;
you are there to improve your physical appearance, health, and your well-being . . . that's all!

> **Note**: When at
> the gym, don't
> be shy to ask for
> help! There are
> trainers on site,
> who are more
> than happy to
> assist you.

How Much Rest Between Sets?

I suggest that you use your resting period between sets to stretch the body part
you are exercising. For example, if you are doing a chest exercise, do a chest
stretching exercise. Do a stretch for 15 seconds and rest for 15 seconds, then
return to the next set.

2: Aerobic Exercise

What Does Cardiovascular Training Do That Strength Training Doesn't?

Cardiovascular training is defined by its ability to elevate your heart rate, which
strengthens the heart muscle so that it circulates blood more efficiently and
delivers fresh oxygen to your muscles and organs.

Clearly, anything that's good for your heart is good for your overall health
and longevity, and cardio fitness is a defense against heart disease.

But that isn't all. If you've ever experienced the endorphin rush that follows
a good workout, you know that there's nothing more exhilarating. It can literally lift the dark curtain of anxiety and depression by delivering the right neurotransmitters to your cells.

Although you can go to a gym and ride a bike, run on a treadmill, use the
Stairmaster, or take an aerobics class, you can also raise your heart rate simply
by walking, bike riding, dancing, or playing a game of tennis.

How Do I Know if I'm Working Hard Enough to Raise My Heart Rate?

Because different people may have different resting heart rates or may find it difficult to take their own heart rate, I use a scale based on your rate of perceived exertion—or RPE—to help you determine the intensity of your cardio training.

Your exercise should be enjoyable, stimulating, and energizing so that you actually look forward to it, rather than dreading it. Working too hard is one of the primary reasons people stop exercising altogether. That said, you don't want to be wasting your time by doing too little, because if you don't begin seeing results, that, too, might lead to your giving up.

My cardio program is based on interval training, which means that you'll be doing 90 seconds at easy/low intensity (such as walking), followed by 30 seconds at relatively high intensity (jogging, running, or walking at an incline). Your easy/low intervals should be at a 3 or 4 on the scale below; the high intensity intervals should be at an 8 or 9. I don't recommend that you ever go beyond a 9.

If you've been sedentary up to this point, I recommend that you keep your intensity levels between a 3 and a 6. You can then increase them as you build strength and endurance.

RPE 1 and 2: Very easy; you can carry on a conversation with no effort
RPE 3: Easy; you can carry on a conversation with almost no effort
RPE 4: Moderately easy; you can talk with minimal effort
RPE 5: Moderate; talking requires some effort
RPE 6: Moderately difficult; talking requires quite a bit of effort
RPE 7: Difficult; conversation requires a lot of effort
RPE 8: Very difficult; conversation requires maximum effort
RPE 9 and 10: Maximum effort; conversation is impossible

Stop exercising immediately if you feel any of the following:

- Chest discomfort, such as pressure or burning
- Chest discomfort radiating to the shoulders or down the arms
- Extreme dizziness, weakness, or disorientation
- Extreme shortness of breath or difficulty breathing

Note: Because you've just finished your strength-training exercises, your heart rate will already be elevated and you'll be warmed up when you start the cardio part of your routine. You can use whatever type of cardio equipment you prefer—a treadmill, bike, stair-climber, elliptical or a cross-trainer. Or you can simply walk, jog, or run.

Interval Training—The Ultimate Cardio Workout

Interval training is my favorite way to boost endorphins and burn fat. It means changing the level of intensity at which you're working out every 90 seconds, which allows you to push yourself harder than if you were working at a higher level of intensity for a longer period of time.

During your 15-minute cardio workout, try walking at a low pace for 90 seconds, and then increase your pace for the 30 seconds before slowing down again. Or, if you're on a stationary bicycle, pedal at a slow pace 90 seconds, then increase the resistance for 30 seconds, and so on. Always start at super low intensity. You can build up the speed or resistance of your intervals so that with each high-intensity segment you'll be working yourself harder than you did the previous time. For example:

- Work at an RPE of 3 for 90 seconds. (You should already be warmed up to this level after your strength training.)
- Increase to an RPE of 6 for the next 30 seconds.
- Slow down to an RPE of 4 for 90 seconds.
- Increase to an RPE of 7 for the next 30 seconds.
- Repeat cycle three times.
- Cool down with 3 minutes at an RPE of 3.

Note: Depending on how fit you are, you may need longer than 30 seconds to come down to an RPE of 4. That's OK! Just keep up with your routine and you'll improve your numbers—and your fitness!

That's your total 15 minutes. To increase your RPE:

- On a treadmill: increase or decrease the incline OR increase or decrease the speed.
- On an elliptical cross-trainer: increase or decrease the resistance.
- On an upright or recumbent stationary bicycle: increase or decrease the speed OR increase or decrease the resistance.
- On a stair-climber: increase or decrease the speed OR increase or decrease the resistance.
- On a rowing machine: increase or decrease the resistance.

Alternative to the Rate of Perceived Exertion

If you're finding the method above a little too technical, simply walk fast or uphill for 30 seconds, then slow your pace down for 90 seconds. Repeat the cycle six times, followed by a three-minute cooldown.

Watch Out for Symptoms of Overtraining

You need to be aware of how you feel in order to determine if you are overtraining. What's too much for you may be just right or too little for the next person. The only one who can know how you feel is *you*!

Some of the most common warning signs of overtraining are:

- Loss of appetite
- Increased irritability
- Pain in the muscles or joints
- Lack of energy
- Insomnia
- Headaches
- Inability to relax
- Increased thirst, dehydration
- Lack of desire to work out (assuming you had the desire in the first place)
- Increased incidence of injury

Note: If you are experiencing several of these symptoms at once, you should see a doctor to rule out any potentially serious cause. Otherwise, just take a few days off to rest, drink plenty of fluids, and adjust your diet if necessary. If you don't get massages on a regular basis, this would be a good time to have one (or two). A good massage will help to flush toxins from your system and loosen you up if your muscles are overworked and/or tense. Get plenty of sleep and resume your workouts when you feel mentally and physically able.

Warming Up and Cooling Down

What you do before you begin and after you complete your workout is as important for your overall health and fitness as the workout itself.

Before beginning your strength-training routine, you need to perform a short warm-up routine. You can do this by walking in place while swinging your arms or, if you're in a gym, using any cardio machine—such as a treadmill set at a moderate pace—for three minutes.

Cooling down is just as important as warming up because it allows your heart rate and breathing to gradually return to normal levels. Otherwise, you might experience the dizziness that results from blood pooling in the large muscles of the legs when vigorous activity is stopped too abruptly. That's why I ask you to finish your cardio workout at an RPE of 2 or 3 for the last 90 seconds, or until your heart rate falls below 100 bpm (beats per minute).

Warm Up Your Mind, along with Your Body

While you're warming up your muscles, do the following to make sure that your mind and body are in sync, and that both are working to help you achieve your goals.

- Think of how you want to look. Imagine your ideal body. How would you look if you could literally manifest that body?

- Imagine all the muscles you are about to work. Feel them, see them chiseled and strong. See your waistline slim. How do you feel mentally, physically, and emotionally?
- Accept those feelings and that appearance as your reality. Act as if you were already fit and strong.

The next 30 minutes are going to be all about you, so focus positively on yourself!

3: Flexibility

Stretching between each set of strength exercises will improve your flexibility and increase your range of motion; it will also increase blood flow to your muscles and break down the buildup of lactic acid that can make you stiff and sore.

Clients often ask me whether doing Pilates or yoga is as effective as strength training. My answer is that for improving muscle tone and promoting fat loss, a combination of strength training and cardiovascular exercise works best. Pilates and yoga can, however, enhance your other workouts by increasing flexibility and core strength.

Pilates is a technique that revolves around using a series of controlled movements designed to improve the strength and flexibility of your body. Being flexible increases your range of motion, which in turn helps your muscles to function better and decreases your chance of injuring yourself. Both yoga and Pilates also engage your mind and body.

The Key to Proper Stretching

- Work into your stretch slowly—don't bounce! Breathe in deeply through your nose.
- Hold your stretch for 10 to 15 seconds to give your muscles time to loosen up.
- As you complete your stretch, exhale through your nose, which will give you a deeper, more complete freedom of motion.

Best Time to Work Out

The best time of the day to workout varies from one individual to another. The important thing is to choose a time of day you can stick with, so that exercise becomes a ritual. Try to work out in the morning for a couple of weeks, then try the afternoon, then the early evening. Which do you enjoy most, and which makes you feel best after your exercise session? I personally prefer mornings because that's when my willpower muscle is at its optimal. I usually exercise at 7 a.m., because no matter how well intentioned I am, if I don't exercise in the morning other things will get in the way. Also, training in the morning induces an increase in the body's metabolism more than any other time of the day. People who do morning sessions start the day with more energy. The production of endorphin helps you get into a better mood, hence the ability to keep a positive attitude throughout the day. Some research suggests that exercising after 3 p.m. can hinder sleep, but I'm a bit skeptical about that one. I guess it depends on the individual and what works best for your lifestyle.

Starting with Two Days a Week

I strongly recommend that you consult with your physician if you are new to strength training or have never exercised before. My recommendation is to start your plan with just two days a week for two weeks, then three times a week for a few weeks, then bump it up to five times a week—if you can! If you are unable to, then just stick with three days a week, every other day.

Remember to warm up for three minutes before you begin. You will be doing two sets of each exercise:

- One set of 15 repetitions with moderate weight
- One set of 12 repetitions with heavier weight (add 5 to 10 pounds)

The only exception to this is the abdominal exercises, for which you need to do 20 to 30 repetitions.

Make sure the last three repetitions of each set require a challenging effort if the weight 20 to 30 repetitions is correct. As you gain strength and your sets no longer seem as challenging, gradually increase the sets to four and increase the weight by 5 to 10 pounds.

Do the appropriate stretch for 15 seconds and rest for 15 seconds between sets.

Increase the intensity of your workout to burn more calories.

Keep the Flame Burning

If you think that exercising is boring, difficult, or something you'd just plain rather skip, I've got news for you: Sometimes I feel that way, too!

But when I do, I use what I call the Aikido method of shifting my thoughts, which is to acknowledge, accept, and let go. The basis of Aikido is to vanquish your opponent (in this case, your lazy or negative thought) by grabbing it (your acknowledgment), pulling it toward you (accepting), and

Note: If you haven't exercised in a while, or if you're changing the way you exercise (so that you're using different muscles), it's normal to feel some muscle soreness within the next 12 to 48 hours. You may also feel some muscle fatigue, stiffness, or weakness, but don't worry about it! As your muscles adapt to the new stress, they'll grow stronger and the soreness will be a thing of the past. Meanwhile, if you're feeling sore, treat yourself to a nice, hot bath—it's much better than taking an ibuprofen.

letting go by throwing it to the side. When you throw your negative thought to the side, you'll make room in your mind for a positive thought to replace it. By doing that, you're adding fuel to the fire of your passion. If you remember what's fueling your heart's desire, you'll find the source of your own passion so that you can use it to keep your flame burning bright.

A Word of Caution

Although there are many forms of strength training programs, as mentioned earlier, modalities such as HIIT training, CrossFit, PX90, Insanity, and many other intense workouts can be downright dangerous if you are just starting out.

I can't say that I've tried all these training modalities, but many of my clients have. Some liked them and many others didn't. I personally prefer to stick to more traditional workouts; those I know to be safe and effective. After all, three decades of experience in the health and fitness industry have taught me a thing or two and when it comes to exercising: always choose what works and what's safe for your body, as it's the only way to reap long lasting results.

Stay clear of injury (no matter what exercise modality you choose):

- Consult with a physician before beginning any exercise regimen.
- Be smart and get rid of your ego-driven self.
- Always listen to your body. For that, you'll have to be mindful of any weird emotional or physical feelings you are experiencing.
- Keep hydrated by sipping water during exercise and drink plenty of fluids after strenuous exercise. This will help to dilute your urine and flush any substance that is released from your muscles out of your kidneys.

Note: I also recommend that you reward yourself with a "cheat day" as you reach a new plateau every two to three weeks, not only so that you can enjoy the process but also because it will help to boost your metabolism. The principle here is the same—your vacation will be a time to rejoice in your progress and also give your body time to rest.

Every 12 Weeks, Give Yourself a Vacation

Remember that 12 weeks is the length of time it will take for your new way of life to become automatic. When you reach that point, take a week off. Taking that time will actually allow your body and mind to come back stronger and with more determination, so remember to "take a break" to completely rejuvenate every three months.

I regularly offer wellness retreats to uncover and eliminate the underlying causes of emotional, mental, and physical stress.

Reach Your Peak of Fitness One Small Step at a Time

Those who have conquered Mt. Everest and Mt. Kilimanjaro got to the summit one small step at a time. They climbed and they rested, climbed and rested, celebrating each new plateau along the way. And when they got to the top, they were rewarded with a limitless vista and a belief in their ability to achieve virtually anything. I urge you to think of your own journey to health and well-being the same way. And know that you, too, can *and* will reach the peak and revel in what you've achieved.

CHAPTER THIRTEEN

GOLDEN RULE #5: YOGA
MORE THAN AN EXERCISE ROUTINE—
IT'S A WAY OF LIFE

"Positive energy generated by love and peace creates healing and builds a gateway to the soul."

IN SOME CULTURES, yoga is a way of life. It is said that this ancient tradition can be traced back more than five thousand years ago, though its philosophy is still embraced by millions around the world. Among the many types of yoga, Kundalini and Vinyasa are the ones I've personally practiced—and still do today.

Every yoga asana (pose) has a different name and includes standing postures, seated twists, backbends, arm balances, inversions, and core holds. For example, the downward facing dog is said to calm the brain, energize the body, strengthen arms and legs, and improve blood pressure. While most postures provide their own benefits, the practice of yoga as a whole offers great health advantages.

Positive effects of *yoga* on productivity, health, and well-being are:

- Increased flexibility
- Increased muscle strength and tone
- Maintaining a balanced metabolism
- Weight reduction
- Injury protection

- Improved energy and vitality
- Cardiovascular health
- Enhances athletic performance

The sun salutation pose (Surya Namaskar), an ancient yoga practice, is a flowing series of 12 poses that help improve strength and flexibility. It is also great for toning the abdominal region. The sequence can be found on YouTube.

Note: You can add this routine to the strength and cardio plans covered in this book, or simply use it as a substitute to your strength training routine. I recommend adding it once a week to your *exercise ritual*. Execute 2 rounds per session.

Golden Rule #6: Massage for Renewal and Rejuvenation

The hands of another are treasures to the soul.

Massage is the oldest and simplest form of medical care. For many centuries, massage has been proven to be an integral part of a healthy lifestyle. In fact, it is one of the oldest healing arts. Some Egyptian tomb paintings show people being massaged. In Eastern cultures, massage has been practiced since ancient times. For centuries, Chinese have been using massage for all sorts of medical conditions. Western research is now confirming that massage isn't just for muscle pain.

Having a massage is one of my favorite ways to relax and rejuvenate. This is an absolute must for many reasons as I outline below. I personally like Thai and deep tissue massages, but many other forms are available and are equally beneficial.

There is no doubt that having a massage makes you feel great. Even a deep tissue sports massage makes you feel wonderful afterward. Massage can help you relieve stress, calm your nervous system, improve clarity, recover from strenuous activity or injury, and even reduce anxiety. It can have a positive effect on muscle toning and consequently increase your ability to control or lose weight.

Positive effects of massage on productivity, health, and well-being are:

- Improved circulation and the supply of nutrition to the muscles by increasing blood flow, which helps them grow and burn more calories as a result.

- Improved immune system. Some studies have measured the stress hormone cortisol in subjects' saliva before and after massage sessions and found a substantial decrease. Cortisol, which is produced by the adrenal gland, kills cells that are important to your immune system. Cortisol is also linked to weight gain and belly fat.

- Improved muscles' range of motion and flexibility. This allows them to maintain greater power and maximum performance while active.

- Shortens the recovery time needed between your workouts. Waste products such as lactic and carbonic acid buildup in muscles during and after exercise.

- Reduces the chance of overtraining. Massage has a relaxing effect on your body and a sedative effect on your nervous system. By helping your recovery, which is paramount to any exercise program, massage can reduce the risk of overtraining, which can limit your ability to build strong healthy muscles and hindering in your ability to burn fat.

- Aids in fat loss. According to some research studies, massage is thought to be able to burst the fat capsule in subcutaneous tissue so that the fat is exuded and becomes absorbed. Combined with proper nutrition and exercise, massage may enhance weight loss and well-being.

Massage may also be helpful for:

- Clarity
- Fibromyalgia
- Anxiety
- Stress-related insomnia
- Headaches
- Joint pain
- Blood circulation

- Digestive issues
- Injuries
- Muscle strain
- Energy increase
- Concentration and focus

Risks of Massage

For many people, massage can be beneficial. However, massage is not appropriate if you have:

- Burns or healing wounds
- Bone fractures
- Blood clots
- Severe osteoporosis
- Severe thrombocytopenia

Please discuss the pros and cons of massage with your physician or healthcare specialist, especially if you are pregnant or have a serious medical condition.

After a massage, or even the next day, you may feel a bit sore. While this is completely normal, massages should not normally be uncomfortable or painful. If any part of your massage doesn't feel right, speak to your therapist. Most problems come from exaggerated pressure during massage, or which they are more than amenable in adjusting (just ask!).

Massage therapy is just as important as exercising and eating healthy. It can contribute to your overall health and well-being. In my 10-year tenure as the fitness and wellness director at a world-class resort, I have witnessed the many positive effects of massage therapy.

Note: I recommend a deep tissue massage. Ideally, try to have one massage a month.

Golden Rule #7:
Sauna: Sweat It Off and Feel Rejuvenated

As the Finnish proverb says, "a sauna is a poor man's pharmacy." I totally agree with that statement! One of my father's beloved rituals was to go to the sauna every Sunday. When I was around ten years old, he would take me with him to the free hot baths and sauna managed by the city of Roubaix, France. I've learned a lot from his wisdom. My dad was a hardworking person, and so spending time together was a rare luxury—and the sauna was our special place to bond. I remember that I had a love-hate relationship with the heat; the only way I could stand it was to get enchanted by the stories he told about our ancestors, the Berbers. We would also get ice cream afterward, which was a welcomed treat. Being in the sauna brought warmth and joy to my body, and listening to dad gave me hope and inspiration.

Nostalgia apart, let's talk about how having a sauna a couple of days a week can help your health and well-being. Your skin is the biggest organ of your body, and is also an important eliminative system. Having a sauna helped me with my preparations while competing for most of my national and international contests, including the Mr. France, Mr. Europe, Mr. World, and Mr. Universe championships.

Saunas helped me eliminate unnecessary water under my skin, get rid of toxins, and feel refreshed after a hard workout. Among the many health benefits, saunas have long been known to help improve the circulation, detoxify the body, and decrease stress. However, just as you would with any piece of equipment, you must be a responsible user of saunas to ensure you don't do any damage to yourself through excessive overuse or improper use.

Warning: You must consult with your physician if you have a history of heart disease. Pregnant women should not spend any time in a sauna at any stage of their pregnancy. People who are using prescription medications should consult with their physicians before using a sauna.

A sauna can be very relaxing and help relieve sore muscles (especially in your back) and joints. Unfortunately, this experience needs to be limited to a safe amount of time. It's recommended that sauna use is limited to 15 to 20 minutes at a time. It's important that users of saunas remain hydrated, as it will produce a lot of sweating, which drains the body of minerals and water. The rule of thumb when using a sauna is to trust your instincts. If you begin to feel overly tired, dizzy, and nauseous—or just feel "off"—it's time to step out of the sauna back into the fresh air.

Positive effects of sauna on productivity, health, and well-being are:

- Improved cardiovascular function
- Lowered blood pressure
- Increased metabolism
- Increased blood flow to the brain
- Increased blood circulation
- Increased relaxation
- Improved weight loss
- Improved sleep
- Decreased stress
- Toxin release
- Improved skin health
- Decreased pain

Note: Have a 10- to 15-minute sauna or steam bath two to three times a week.

Voilà! Now you have all the necessary and powerful tools you need to be on a path to long lasting health and well-being.

EPILOGUE:

DON'T GIVE UP: "DESIRE TO FIGHT"

Keep On, Keeping On

IN THE PREVIOUS chapters, we have talked at length about self-worth, trust, tranquility, and the body. We have explored in depth the importance of cultivating them in order to put yourself in the field of possibilities. To live to your full potential, yes, it is essential that you know how to have a worthy life, have a trustful mindset, be tranquil and calm, and, of course, take care of your body. But out of all of this, the indictors of success are resilience, persistence, and grit. Call it what you want, I call it a "desire to fight." I was born fighting. I don't like to take no for an answer, and am a firm believer that, as the old saying goes, "If there's a will, there's always a way." My family's story is a testament to this.

On July 1, 1962, a caravan of French army trucks left my family's tent camp in Roumana, Algeria, for the city of M'Sila. The trucks carried a group of former nomads of the Ouled Khaled tribe, including my parents. My father was twenty-nine years old and my newly married mother, who was fifteen years old and six months pregnant, were in the back crossing the Sahara, enduring the heat, rutted roads, and inscrutable silence of my grandfather. Trauma was the fabric of my family's life. My grandfather had already been incapacitated by humiliation and violence. The French occupied Algeria, and in 1950 forcibly settled my tribe in the camps of Ben Srour, requiring them to give up their way of life and traditions. When my grandfather resisted, his fourteen-year-old son, my uncle, was captured and made to endure electric shock to his genitals. My father was only spared the same treatment because my quick-thinking grand-mother hid him in a hole in the ground and sat on top of it, pretending to bake bread, as the French army ransacked their tent looking for him. My grandfather had every right to be cautious.

An hour into the journey, my mother called out in pain. Terrified and screaming, she realized she was going into early labor. Everyone persuaded the driver to stop at the only acacia tree they could see. As soon as the truck reached the tree, I was born, blue faced, and frighteningly small. My grandfather pulled out his ancient pocketknife and cut the umbilical cord. He had lived and seen enough tragedy to know I would not survive. He took off his *gandoura* and wrapped me in it. My exhausted teenage mother held me and wept, hoping that my crying—incessant and noisy for such a tiny thing—was proof of health and a will to live.

The women of the tribe were worried and came to a consensus: this baby was sickly and would surely die. My mother's tight grip around me didn't convince them. They had seen enough childbirths to recognize when a young mother's hope is futile and unhealthy. They told her what must be done. What tradition called for: a baby with a dubious chance at life should be given back to God. "You must take him to the cemetery and leave him atop a gravestone," they told my mother. "If he stays quiet as you walk away, he was never destined to live." At the cemetery, my mother found herself hysterical with fear, devastated, and preparing herself to abandon her first born. She paced back and forth, holding me close to her, and memorizing my face. All she wanted to do was cover me with kisses. Instead, she looked at my tiny and pale face, and sternly scolded me to *fight*. She then laid me down and backed away slowly, giving me enough time to protest, wail, or fuss. Nothing. Her heart sank, but she had to keep backing away and reminding herself to trust in God and let her son go. But I came to my senses and began to cry. It wasn't a loud cry, but enough for my mother to come back running to me.

No one in my family was surprised when my mother brought me back. When we finally arrived at M'Sila, the clouds of war were still hanging overhead, swarming with soldiers, displaced tribes, and frighten French citizens running for their lives; the area was slowly recovering from the chaos of the devastating French-Algerian War. My parents gathered the last penny they had and took me to the hospital; it was their last hope. The doctor looked at my young parents in their dusty clothes and their fragile baby, with bright red translucent skin, and took me from them to be examined alone. My parents, knowing no better, waited. Finally, he returned, and solemnly informed my mother that her son had just died. And no, the doctors said, you may not see your son or take home the corpse for burial. My mother fell to her knees screaming. My father demanded to see his child, but no, the doctor insisted it was time to go.

In shock and disbelief, my parents went to the police station, grieving and angry. When they showed up at the hospital with a police officer to demand they be allowed to give their child a proper burial, the doctor produced me, alive, muttering a rationale about how no teenage girl should have to raise a chronically ill infant that's bound to die. My mother's face, wet with tears, had some choice words for the doctor. The roller-coaster ride of emotions was too much for my parents to handle, as my mother collapsed in the streets, sobbing with me in her arms, while my father tried his best to comfort the both of us.

Desire to Fight—What Does It Mean?

The story of my birth and my survival as a preemie baby has become part of my family's heritage. When we went through any type of hardship, my mother would repeat my birth story. The message was that we aren't quitters. We don't give up because life is hard or because others are convinced we can't do something or because we have tried enough times. This was always my mentality, too. For years, this was the only way I knew how to live. If I felt someone was undermining my talents, I made it my mission to prove them wrong. I was focused on beating their expectations. The dark side of this was when my family faced threatening situations, we kept our head down. I still vividly remember walking with my father when I was nine to go get groceries when a car pulled up right next to us. A burly young man with a shaved head got out and started yelling and spiting at us. I was terrified. He called us rats—I remember that well. Once he noticed he had frightened us enough, he got back in the car and drove off. My father held out his hand and I put mine in his and we kept walking to the store. We never spoke of it again.

———

It was a hot and humid day in Arizona on September 11, 2001, when two planes flew into the World Trade Center in New York City. Like most Americans, I watched the images of the towers collapsing on TV in complete horror. *How could this happen?* It seemed like a sick and twisted joke the universe was playing on us. I went home, hugged my wife, and tried to grapple with how the world had changed in just one day. The next day when I came into work, I overheard one of my colleagues making disparaging remarks about all Muslims; he basically wanted all of us dead. This would include my hardworking parents, uncles, brothers, and sisters, whose jobs and strengths were varied and as eclectic as they were. All the emotions I felt as a kid rushed back to me. I was terrified. I was confused. But now there was one more layer added: even though I had achieved so much, had become a successful businessman, a respected member of society, I was still an Arab who was going to be discriminated against. I did what my family taught me to do: I kept my head down and worked hard. Actually, I worked harder.

My family had taught me to go into survival mode. Since trauma was a fabric of our life, we were proud of being survivors. We knew how to take the punches and keep rolling. If we felt threatened, the code was to keep trying harder. The only time you fought back is if someone was going to threaten your life. If there was an obstacle, be ingenious, be smart, and find a way around it. I was so proud of what I had been taught. However, when I started digging into the mindset, I actually realized how limiting it was. Rather than thriving at life, I was just surviving. My interaction with the world was passive and very timid. I never felt like I had any worth. Why couldn't I tell my racist colleague that he was wrong? Why didn't my father stand up to the neo-Nazi skinhead? We were taught to diminish our power. If we talked back or questioned an authority figure, we were troublemakers. Even though I worked out and made my body big and strong, I was always trying to take up as little space as possible, both physically and emotionally.

We need to be careful we aren't surviving on someone else's terms. My family white-knuckled it through an awful situation . . . until we came up against the next awful situation. We were always playing defense. Instead, we needed to live life on our own terms.

Once again, before we go any further, we need to define what thriving actually means. For me, thriving in life means living with purpose and meaning. It's being able to find a kernel of wisdom and insight after going through a difficult situation or experiencing failure. I recall a conversation with a breast cancer survivor whom eloquently explained why she preferred being called a thriver and not just a survivor: "In most cases, we don't just survive the cancer. We actually get more tuned into our goals, our family, and our health. We thrive because we know our time is extremely valuable and we no longer have the innocence of thinking that we may have a long healthy life without pitfalls."

Walking away with a lesson makes you an active participant and not a victim. As thrivers, we can learn from every mistake, terrifying incident, and failure. Never again, we can say. Next time this happens, I won't let anyone or anything take advantage of me. Whether that might be cancer, death, racism, an abusive step-parent, or any other obstacle we might have to deal with in our lives.

Thrivers shatter the concept of learned helplessness. In 1965, scientist Martin Seligman, while trying to expand on the findings of Ivan Pavlov, shocked dogs but also provided them an escape from the punishment. He was horrified to find that after a dog was shocked enough times, it actually gave up any attempt at running away from the abuse. It just sat there and took the shock. The implications of this study are horrifying. If you have endured enough abuse and trauma in your life, you are more likely not to escape from it and actually, instead, accept it as reality. Thrivers don't accept the status quo. We don't believe it when we are told we won't amount to very much or that we should play it safe, accepting complacency over pursuing our dreams. In order to reject the status quo and learned helplessness, thrivers live a purposeful life.

Finding your purpose in life is no small feat. In fact, it can take a lifetime. It doesn't help that family, school, and college force us not to listen to our inner guidance or voice. We are cajoled to be sensible with our life choices, and oftentimes end up following someone else's script. How are we supposed to know what our purpose is when we are told not to listen to our inner voice? Jack Canfield, author of *Chicken Soup for the Soul,* uses the metaphor of GPS to help us understand the importance of purpose.

If you get into a car and can't plug your location in and the destination you want to head to, life will be a chaotic mess. To find your purpose, know and understand where you are in life now. What is your current location? Are you working in a job you hate? Do you feel like you are just surviving? When was the last time you felt and experienced joy? Now, where do you want to end up? Visualize your end destination. This is the fun part. In five years or even in the next year, where do you want to be? Do you want to experience joy again? Once you have figured out what your purpose is, stay focused. Thrivers stay focused on their purpose.

Cultivating Thriving Skills

I got lucky. When I was nineteen, I sat in front of the TV in awe as I watched a young gymnast do his routine. He looked powerful while graceful and elegant. I knew immediately that I wanted to be a gymnast, and this first thought eventually lead to my interest in bodybuilding. If I hadn't found my purpose and goal, I would have been an extremely unhappy person. It has not only brought me fame and success, but has also given me so much joy. When I have shared my story with clients, they first find it difficult to understand how to affirm their purpose. Yes, affirm. Your purpose can be pretty obvious, and it just might be a matter of affirming it.

I have borrowed heavily from Jack Canfield to come up with these exercises. Jack has, I believe, done a brilliant job of articulating how to begin finding your purpose. His advice has been eye-opening for me and my clients. If we really break it down, it starts by reliving the three times in your life when you have felt joy, happiness, and a sense of fulfillment.

Write down answers to the following questions:

- When was the last time you have experienced joy and happiness?
- What recent activity or interaction gave you a sense of fulfillment?
- If you could create your own future, what would it look like?

Take your time to write out the answers. Answer them once in the morning, once in the afternoon, and once during the weekend. Make sure you are in the right frame of mind when you are writing out these answers. Once you are satisfied, use your answer to write out your mission statement. Mine is, actually, very simple: "To help people realize their true potential." Nothing brings me more joy and fulfillment than watching people I have met become aware of how strong, capable, and worthy they are. Your mission statement should reflect the kind of life you want to live. It should be used to create the goals you want to achieve in your life.

Being able to articulate your purpose and mission in life is no small feat. While it may take some time, it can eventually be the springboard for you to begin focusing on your goals. Also, it can push you to listen to your inner voice, your gut, and your heart. We have been taught too long to undermine our feelings, wants, and needs. Instead, we are forced to live a very prescribed life. The message continues to be to not stick out, to conform, and to expect very little out of life: go to college, get married, have children, buy a house, work, and retire—this has become the definition of a "good" life. We are actively told not to listen to our heart. It's hard—close to impossible—to know what your purpose is if you aren't listening to what your heart wants. The three simple questions I have offered will hopefully help you trust your gut, heart, and push you to thrive instead of just survive.

Once you have a purpose, and when it's married with your self-worth, you can begin to feel empowered. The status quo won't bother you. The social restrictions people want to impose on you will seem small and easy to break.

You won't need to survive by fitting into the roles someone else has created for you. It's one of the most liberating feelings you can experience. As someone who has seen clients realize they have power to create their own self, I can tell you the change is pretty immediate; their shoulders become broader and they walk into a room with conviction and intention. No more waiting for the punch and going with the flow. No more just being a survivor.

Hope, Thrivers, and Infinite Possibilities

"Hope is being able to see that there's light despite all the darkness."
—Desmond Tutu

I don't think we talk enough about hope in society. When I wake up in the morning, I revel in my feelings of hopefulness. A lot of thinkers, psychologists, and researchers believe hope is a crutch. It's not rooted in any sort of reality, they say. It's easy to sit at home and hope for a better life or someone who is going to rescue you from your current situation. They like to argue it isn't very practical. It doesn't force you to get your life in order or be active in creating your power. But the opposite of hope—hopelessness—is devastating to experience and feel. If you have experienced hopelessness, the sentences you will start to believe are, "I feel like giving up," "I have no future," "It's too late now." When I worked with Alzheimer's patients who had given up on life and were hopeless, it was very hard to convince them their life was meaningful and worthy. There was a dense air of dread and gloominess. My heart would break for these patients. There was no convincing them that, even with their disease, they could live a full life. Even the doctors would have done anything to inject even the smallest amount of hope into their patients.

We absolutely need resilience, grit, and persistence . . . but we also need hope. Without hope, there is nothing to look forward to. There is no future for us to believe in. Experiencing hope is not foolhardy. Yes, I agree that hope needs to be matched with action. But when you have the desire to fight and are ready to take the leap, you have to be armed with positivity, optimism, and a sense of hopefulness. It offers us meaning. It helps put into context all the challenges and fear we have experienced, and most likely will in the future. When you are standing on the 40-foot pole getting yourself ready to jump, we can conjure up all the negative thoughts and feelings, but hope is what will motivate us to take the leap. It reminds us that we can change the situation we are currently in. It allows us to imagine a different way of living and meaning.

If there's one thing I wish I could have done for the patients at the Alzheimer's Research & Prevention Foundation, I would have shown them that every day they were alive and breathing they had hope: hope for change, hope for love, hope for new friendships, hope for new experiences, hope for happiness. It offers the ability to imagine the infinite possibilities life can offer. Climbing up the 40-foot pole or swimming out into the open ocean are acts of hope. Believing that change is possible and taking the leap is a defiant act of hope. This is what I humbly offer you in this book: Hope for a new and bright future where you can live out your potential.

AUTHOR'S NOTE PERTAINING TO COVID-19

IN EARLY FEBRUARY 2020, when COVID-19 started in America, this book was already in the process of being edited. Some of my recommendations in this book—such as going out and having fun outdoors—became simply irrelevant during social distancing, stay-at-home orders, and quarantine. It's easy to preach about health, fitness, and wellness under normal circumstances and when we aren't under the constant threat of a virus. But these aren't normal times, so I'm adding some thoughts on how one can seek health and well-being amid challenges. Be mindful that the content outlined in this book will make you stronger, healthier, and happier—which are all powerful tools to boost your immune system and face any challenge.

At this moment, as I write this, it's not over yet.

It has now been eight months. There have been promises of an imminent vaccine, but nothing yet. We're still social distancing and wearing masks. We're still talking on Zoom with colleagues, friends, and family. Kids are still going to class online. Most of us are still exercising at home. Millions are still unemployed. Restaurants and hotels are at half capacity by ordinance, air travel is at a standstill, and the number of cases is still climbing. As of October 2020, and according to the John Hopkins Coronavirus Center, there were 7,711,07 confirmed cases and 214,337 deaths in the US alone. Life has not yet returned to normal.

Stay-at-home and confinement orders had been lifted nationwide a few months ago, but some countries in Europe are mandating lockdowns again as the cases are resurging. Will we have to quarantine again? Not sure. What I do know is that, amid all this chaos, we still have a choice. The choice to stay healthy and stay strong, or the choice to risk it all. The choice to elevate to a higher level of existence or the choice to remain in a state of panic.

I think that, by now, most of us are better equipped to deal with quarantines. We know more, but we also know that prolonged uncertainty can weigh on our overall health and well-being. Fear, doubt, and anxiety about what could happen can be overwhelming and can cause strong emotions in us adults, and in our children as they are susceptible to our own fears. Public health actions—such as social distancing—can make us feel isolated and even traumatized. That's because we aren't meant to stay inside. Movement, fresh air, sun, and the connections with nature—as well as with other human beings—are not only important, but vital to our very existence. However, these actions are necessary to reduce the spread of COVID-19. Respecting the experts' advice will help us to protect each other until this is over.

To cope with stress during quarantine, it's important to keep our brain and body active. Things like scheduling our days in advance to avoid boredom is not such a bad idea, and can make a huge difference. Keeping a busy schedule is the key to remaining healthy.

As I said earlier, pandemics can be traumatic so it's important to be aware of the changes you are experiencing, both mentally and physically.

There are several changes that can be brought on by the COVID-19:

- Fear and worry about your own health, as well as of your friends and family members' health.
- Uncertainty about your financial and job situation.
- Worsening of chronic health problems.
- Difficulty sleeping.
- Difficulty concentrating.
- Increased use of tobacco and/or alcohol and drugs.
- Changes in eating patterns.

If you are experiencing crises, please get immediate help and support from friends, family, or your physician. There are also many helpline resources, such as the MentalHealthFoundation.org, who have tons of information to guide you through crisis.

I personally find that calling or video conferencing with friends and family members to be very effective in helping you feel connected, loved, and less isolated.

"If you fail to understand others, at least don't hurt them!"

The coronavirus pandemic has rear-ended life as we know it while deepening the crevice in an already divided America. Most Americans love their freedom—I know I do—and that sometimes can cause people to overreact and even become violent. It's a huge problem we're facing.

At the root of the problem lies a lack of self-worth, the absence of conscience, and the loss of a moral base that helps guide pro-social behavior. Self-worth, conscience, and a moral base are what lead people to behave in socially acceptable and more humane ways. Without it, some, in a way, are unable to see that their actions are threatening the very stability of the world. This phenomenon isn't new—humans have always been a dangerous and conflicted species. They create their own problems based on erroneous thinking and blame each other for failing to fix them. Conflict resolution then becomes elusive when you have clashing belief systems and conflicting core values.

It's evident that there is a clash of consciousness that fiercely divides America!

On one side, you have those who stand behind their convictions and their constitutional rights—thus ignoring health experts' guidelines and warnings. They want freedom, but take away freedom from others: the freedom to be safe and healthy! And on the other side are those who agree that confinement, quarantine, or any kind of stay at home order is crucial to stop the spread of the virus, which can be critical to humanity's very existence.

As I write, I'm reminded of a quote by Simón Bolívar: "An ignorant people is the blind instrument of its own destruction." I can't find a better way to describe those who refuse to comply with health officials' safety guidelines—or any guidelines that can save lives.

I'm sure that many of you can sympathize with those who abide with the rules—I know I do! But I could also argue for anti-confinement, as I lost my youngest brother of forty-five—not to COVID-19, but *because* of it. He died of one of the other pandemics made worse by confinement—addiction. It had gotten difficult for him to cope with the months of isolation in the south of France. Then, one night, alone and in total distress, he drank himself to death. He was found hours later, lying on the floor of his living room. To make matters worse, 25 members of my family in France tested positive after my little niece contracted the virus at school. It was a nightmare for all of us. Fortunately, they all recovered and are in good health.

Furthermore, two of my best friends lost their mothers, and my literary agent lost her father due to COVID-19. I should be furious at those who downplay the situation and walk around, unprotected, as if there was nothing going on. These are young men and women and older folks alike. Moms and dads with their children shopping in crowded stores, entirely ignoring the social distancing guidelines, and most aren't even wearing a face mask. Even men of God defied stay-at-home orders and kept their churches open to hundreds of worshippers, thus putting them at risk. Those people come from all walks of life; they are intelligent folks—so why are they behaving so dangerously? And most importantly, how can we understand them?

Note: Despite these horrific events, I'm still not anti-confinement! And I still think we must follow proper safety guidelines if we want to win the war against the virus.

Perhaps this quote from one of the pioneers of modern psychology, Carl Jung, can shed some light: "Everything that irritates us about others can lead us to an understanding of ourselves." In other words: if you can see it in others, you have it in you.

As I referred to it earlier, lack of self-worth and the absence of conscience may be causing unnecessary conflicts. We, as human beings, are either stuck in a low level of existence where clarity and awareness are rather clouded by an erroneous belief system fueled by fear, anxiety, and doubt, or thrive on a higher level of existence where we seem to maintain a healthy equilibrium between what I call "The Four Pillars of Mindful Fitness"—the physical, emotional, mental, and spiritual aspects of one's life. When we rise to this higher level, we cultivate a greater sense of clarity and awareness.

One of the definitions for consciousness is "an inner feeling or voice viewed as acting as a guide to the rightness or wrongness of one's behavior."

I'm not a politician, an activist, or mental health professional. I am a human being who works with other human beings in helping them create an optimum state of inner fitness by regaining three life-sustaining components: health, happiness, and love. Ironically, these can only be obtained by reclaiming a sense of self-worth and by rising to a higher level of existence. Anger, reactivity, doubt, fear, and hatred won't get you anywhere except where you already are—stuck at the lowest level of existence.

Nordine Zouareg
October 2020

ACKNOWLEDGMENTS

I would like to express my deepest appreciation to my literary agent Julie Gwinn at The Seymour Agency and my editor Jason Katzman at Skyhorse Publishing for their efforts and patience in making the process of creating this book so much easier. My sincere thanks to Melissa Quesada for her love and support. I would also like to extend my deepest gratitude to Dr. Richard Carmona for taking the time and effort in writing the foreword of this book.

I'd like to acknowledge the team at Skyhorse Publishing for their hard work. I'd also like to extend my thanks to Humberto and Czarina Lopez who never wavered in their support. A sincere thanks to Tatyana Gann for introducing me to my new agent.

And, finally, many thanks to Dr. Dharma Singh Khalsa, Jerry Avenaim, Wyatt Webb, Gurumeet Khalsa, and John Assaraf for their assistance.